WORDS,

"This groundbreaking book takes on an issue of great significance not only to those interested in intercultural communication in Native American relations with non-Indians, but also, and maybe more importantly, it tackles a problem that directly affects the health and well-being of Native Americans in their relationships with medical caregivers. It has practical as well as academic value, and offers insight and strategies for providers as well as thoughtful analysis for scholars engaged in research on linguistics and Native American Studies."—Franke Wilmer, Ph.D., Professor of Political Science, Montana State University; former member Montana House of Representatives; Chair of the Montana Human Rights Commission.

"In this timely, thoroughly researched and beautifully written book, Nancy Lande exposes the critical communication gaps that too often exist between Western-trained medical professionals and American Indians. Her powerful findings inspire a centering of reflexive communication and cultural fluency in all reservation-based health care practices. This book is highly recommended for scholars and practitioners alike." —Leah Schmalzbauer, Ph.D., Associate Professor of Sociology, Anthropology, and American Studies, Amherst College.

"The demographic research and narrated stories elicited by Nancy Lande focus on communicative frustrations that too many Native Americans and their health care providers experience in areas of cultural, social, economic, linguistic, health, and belief practices. Faulty verbal and nonverbal communications clash with the ability to effectively gain patient information, comprehension, and treatment. The issues explored in this book could not be more timely, since minority and Indigenous communities are actively standing against such structural and historic inequities" —Ruth Donegal Burleigh, (1952-2016, Cree) RN/BSN; M.A.; The Friends of the Sweet Grass Hills.

"WORDS, WOUNDS, CHASMS is a major contribution to the scholarship about health care among Indigenous Peoples, not just in Montana, but globally. Well researched and well written, this text by Nancy Lande examines the nature of Native health care needs and contemporary health care practices. She contends, quite correctly, that effective communication between health care providers and patients is complex and becomes more so when cultural and socio-economic strata are included. Lande properly grounds her discussions on the importance of Indigenous Methodologies and the need for the ethical protocol for research with Indigenous communities. This work will be helpful to a wide audience in the health care fields but particularly valuable to those engaged in health disparity scholarship among Native peoples." — Walter C. Fleming, (Kickapoo) Ph.D., Department Head and Professor of Native American Studies, Montana State University; past President of the National Indian Counselors' Association; past Chair of Humanities Montana; and past Vice President of the Montana Chapter of the American Civil Liberties Association.

"I am a physician who has been teaching leadership to other physicians (interns, residents, and especially chief residents) for over four decades. During that time, I have trained over 20,000 aspiring young physicians. The essential message has remained true throughout various courses and seminars. To maximize the effectiveness of interpersonal communication, everyone (deliverer as well as recipient) must aspire to better understand the source of the recipient's reception of health communications. Creating an effective doctor-patient relationship alone is fraught with peril, but the addition of major cross cultural differences makes generating such effective relationships almost impossible. Nancy Lande's work reveals some of the sources of these difficulties and, as such, is a significant contribution to that conversation." —Robert A. Doughty, M.D., Ph.D.; Multiple Hospital and Research positions as Physician, Faculty, and Administrator; The Alfred I. duPont Institute and Vice President of Physician Practices for The Nemours Foundation; Senior Scholar for Experiential Learning and Leadership Development, Accreditation Council for Graduate Medical Education and Professor of Pediatrics.

WORDS, WOUNDS, CHASMS

NATIVE AMERICAN
HEALTH CARE ENCOUNTERS

2nd Edition

Also by Nancy Lande

HOMESCHOOLING: A PATCHWORK OF DAYS
SHARE A DAY WITH 30
HOMESCHOOLING FAMILIES

HOMESCHOOL OPEN HOUSE
Interviews with 55 Families

WORDS, WOUNDS, CHASMS
Native American Health Care Encounters
1st Edition

WORDS, WOUNDS, CHASMS

NATIVE AMERICAN
HEALTH CARE ENCOUNTERS
2nd Edition

NANCY LANDE

WindyCreek Press
Bozeman, Montana

DEDICATION

With Deepest Gratitude
to

Alexander Saxton
Emeritus Professor of History—UCLA
Founder of Asian American Studies Center—UCLA
historian, novelist, activist, dear friend and mentor
whose nurture and trust he handed over
with a twinkle in his eye.
(1919-2012)

Diana Eades
Adjunct Professor in Linguistics—
University of New England, Australia
whose seminal works in critical sociolinguistics
and intercultural communication inspired this
investigation for her support
and encouragement.

Noam Chomsky
"The Father of Modern Linguistics,"
Institute Professor and Emeritus Professor
of Linguistics—MIT,
philosopher, cognitive scientist,
historian, social critic, and political activist
for reshaping linguistic structures
and relentlessly fighting
for social justice.

"The traditions of our people are handed down from father to son. The Chief is considered to be the most learned, and the leader of the tribe. The Doctor, however, is thought to have more inspiration. He is supposed to be in communion with spirits. . . . He cures the sick by the laying of hands, and payers and incantations and heavenly songs. He infuses new life into the patient, and performs most wonderful feats of skill in his practice. . . . He clothes himself in the skins of young innocent animals, such as the fawn, and decorated himself with the plumage of harmless birds, such as the dove and hummingbird . . ."

— Sarah Winnemucca Paiute (1844-1891)

"How smooth must be the language of the Whites, when they can make right look like wrong, and wrong like right."

—From Black Hawk, Sauk

"Basically, I have only one object of historical study, that is the threshold of modernity. Who are we, we who speak a language such that it has powers that are imposed on us in our society as well as on other societies? What is this language which can be turned against us which we can turn against ourselves? What is this incredible obsession with the passage to the universal in Western discourse? That is my historical problem."

—Michel Foucault, (2004). Quote for December 2007

"I think the use of language is a very important means by which this species, because of its biological nature, creates a kind of social space, to place itself in interactions with other people. It doesn't have much to do with communication in a narrow sense; that is, it doesn't involve transmission of information. There is much information transmitted but it is not the content of what is said that is transmitted. There is undoubtedly much to learn about the social uses of language, for communication or for other purposes."

—Noam Chomsky, in W. Osiatynski (1984)

CONTENTS

ACKNOWLEDGMENTS

Diana Eades utilized a sociolinguistic approach and analysis of observed and/or recorded interactions of ways Aboriginal Australians who speak varieties of English struggle to communicate in the legal process due to differing uses of English. Aboriginal problems of navigating the legal field parallel situations linked to my own interest regarding Native Americans who face miscommunications that affect their health care. I built on Diana's research as the scaffolding on which to base my own investigation. She was enthusiastic and encouraged me to design a study that would uncover and frame similar underling concerns of miscommunications in the critical area of health care for Native Americans. For all of her efforts and encouragement, I am truly grateful.[1]

I have many professors to thank for their friendship, assistance, advice, disciplinary expertise and long-term support in their various academic fields. SOCIOLOGY: Robin Wagner-Pacifici (Swarthmore College; University of Exile Professor; New School of Social Research) and Leah Schmalzbauer (Sociology, Anthropology, and American Studies; Amherst College). HISTORY: Alexander Saxton (1919-2012, founder of the nation's first Asian American Studies program; Professor Emeritus UCLA), and Margaret Connell-Szasz (American Indian Education, Comparative Indigenous Education and History; Regents Professor University of New Mexico). POLITICAL SCIENCE: Franke Wilmer (former member Montana House of Representatives; Montana State University). ENGLISH/LINGUISTICS: Diana Eades (University of New England, Australia), and Phil Gaines (Discourse Analysis, Forensic Linguistics; Montana State University). NATIVE AMERICAN STUDIES: Walter Fleming (Kickapoo; past President of the National Indian Counselors' Association, past Chair of the Montana Committee for the Humanities, and past Vice President of the Montana Chapter of the Ameri-

---

[1] Diana Eades serves with the Communication of Rights Group that has released Guidelines for Communicating Rights to Non-Native Speakers of English in Australia, England and Wales, and the USA These guidelines can be found online at: http://www.une.edu.au/__data/assets/pdf_file/0006/114873/Communication-of-rights.pdf; November, 2015.

can Civil Liberties Association, Department Head of Native American Studies; Montana State University) and Wayne Stein (Turtle Mountain Chippewa; Montana State University). AMERICAN STUDIES: Gerald Vizenor, (Chippewa; UC Berkeley Emeritus; University of New Mexico), Amanda Cobb-Greetham (Chickasaw; Coca Cola Professor and Director of the Native American Studies Program; University of Oklahoma College of Arts and Sciences), and M. Jane Young (Emeritus Professor; University of New Mexico).

The Tribal Leaders and Unit Directors at various reservations and Indian Health Services (IHS) in Montana had trust in me that allowed me access to doctors, nurses, pharmacists, aides, counselors, staff, and patients in their facilities, who all took time to give forthright and insightful answers to my questions because of their general awareness of significant communicative problems. Thank you. My gratitude to Terry Dennis at the Billings IHS area office who made sure to provide the brochure I created (that highlighted the communicative problems isolated in my study) to clinicians and patients at IHS facilities in Montana. I would also like to express my sincere gratitude and respect to the many Native American participants who graciously stopped in their tracks, often at clinics, hospitals, or social events, with children or relatives at their side, to talk about how the nature of health communications affects their care. I truly value the relationships that flourished with many of my Native American friends, colleagues, students, and tribal members across the state who shared their stories and were willing to confide in me. Special thanks to Mitzi Griffin, who so graciously, generously, and enthusiastically transcribed all of the narrative interviews.

Personal thanks to my dear Native friends Ruth Burleigh (1952-2012), Alice Baker, and Shane Doyle for their passion, access, hospitality, life lessons, feedback, and excitement about this work.

I am most grateful to my husband, Gary, who is my truest friend and supporter. As a physician, he has worked on the problematic of doctor-patient relationships for decades. He is genuinely interested in my work, which is extremely sustaining. I love him most for his generosity, huge heart, synthesis of all matters of the mind, spirit, imagination, and for his time. He has endlessly been my listener, reader, responder, and supporter for this project and all the other aspects of my life.

I
INTRODUCTION

Personally, I don't like doctors. I don't trust doctors. I don't trust anyone in the health care profession. A lot of it has been with my personal experience with 'em. You know, to me, they're nothing but used car salesmen. All of 'em. You know, and yeah it's supposed to be the greatest job in the world. That's fine, you know, but for me, I'm gonna stay healthy. You know, I've watched three of my relatives die in the hospital over the past four years—my grandmother and two uncles. Two afflicted with cancer. My grandmother, she was 90 years old, and I guess you could say natural causes, but in not one, in any of those three instances, did I really feel like the hospital is where they should be. I felt like it's very impersonal at the hospital, you're just a number, you know. They miss things all the time. They don't have enough time to see every patient. These doctors can't do everything they should for all these patients because they've got too many. They got, money is an issue, all these different issues come up, and so I guess I do believe that there's a failure of communication and I think it has to do with the fact that hospitals is very impersonal places and patients aren't given the human dignity that they deserve as a human being. Rather they're just kind of seen as a customer or, you know, a patient. So, yeah, that's how I feel. —Alan (Indian patient)

The narrative above speaks volumes about Indians[2] who seek health care at Montana reservation health facilities. Indian patients often struggle with feeling depersonalized, misunderstood, and disrespected. Patients and clinicians can also be frustrated by miscommunications in health care encounters due to "invisible" cultural and linguistic divides, which are the central foci of this investigation.

---

[2] North American Indian, American Indian, and Native American are all terms used by non-Indians to refer to the Indigenous Peoples of the United States. Throughout the interviews and conversations collected for this book, Native people in Montana routinely refer to themselves and each other as Indians. Thus, Indian is the term that is most often used.

Indian patients initially go to a clinic to seek help. But help isn't always the outcome of the visit. Because English is the shared language for health conversations, it does not necessarily mean that Indians and non-Indian clinicians actually share the same comprehensions, values, or functions. Language is expressed as both the production and the reception of verbal and non-verbal cues that are natural within any particular cultural setting. Indians living on reservations have significantly different cultures and practices than mainstream Western[3] societies. Sociolinguistics is an approach and analysis of ways Indians who speak varieties of English struggle to communicate about health care. Indian words, gestures, and conversations often deliver entirely different meanings to their Non-Indian clinicians' than the meanings patients had intended. Similarly, communications from clinician to patient are also often misunderstood by patients. Clinicians[4] who have stayed at Indian Health Service (IHS)[5] facilities for years and made it a point to know the people, however, have experienced more informed and successful communications with their patients than those who regularly rotate through in short periods of time and don't study or get involved with the community.

Clinicians are well versed in the speech patterns of Western culture and biomedicine.[6] Language is the specific expression of any culture or microculture, whether Indian, minority, immigrant, ethnic, religious, generational, professional, etc. The field of sociolinguistics studies communications where meaning, language, culture,

---

[3] It is nearly impossible to phrase a term to describe the cultural group that originated in Europe and also eventually formed the majority population of much of North America, Australia, and New Zealand. The term Western will be used in reference to these First World cultures and to White Caucasians in the United States.

[4] The term clinician refer to a combination of doctors, nurses, counselors, emergency personnel, pharmacists, and other medical professionals and administrators so as not to reveal specific identifying information of those interviewed.

[5] Refer to Chapter 2 for further information about IHS facilities.

[6] Biomedicine refers to a branch of medical science that applies biological, physiological, and other natural science concepts to clinical practices and had been the principle health system for well over a century. See following sections on Biomedicine in the Introduction and Chapter 2.

worldview, and socio-economic influences intersect, and it articulates how languages relate to social factors that include differences such as region, class, dialects, gender, racial stereotypes, and bilingualism.

There is a paucity of research related to linguistics and health beliefs regarding health practices on the material settings of Indian reservations in Montana (the geographic focus of this inquiry). Since the clinician-patient relationship is always a result of habitus[7] (individual, linguistic, and cultural dispositions and enactments of worldview), socioeconomics as they impact identity, culture, language, health care, and biomedicine. The nature of the Indian Health Service (IHS)[8] and its practices reflect a complex structure that clinical professionals, administrators, staff, and Indian patients must navigate while addressing health care at reservation facilities.

An explorative field approach and ethnographically structured interviews were the methods used to collect qualitative data based on a predetermined set of questions regarding sociolinguistic (verbal and nonverbal) miscommunications. The focus on communications was informed by a review of literature that helped to connect relationships of Indigenous sociolinguistics, habitus, worldview, tribal culture, health care, biomedicine, socio-economic conditions, and health belief systems in order to understand what disrupts experiences of feeling good about health care.

---

[7] Pierre Bourdieu characterizes habitus as containing the meaning of habitat, habitant, and the process of habitation and habit (particularly habits of thought). Habitat is the lived social environment, as exemplified by the product of its position in the social space as well as the practices that the social beings that inhabit it carry out. The social space is a multidimensional map of the social order: economic, cultural and symbolic capital, education, class, and historical paths that is the main axes around which social order is articulated. Since these paths are not separate, habitus is simultaneously a position in the social and historical flow; a practice within the position and its flow; and a social identity or the habitus of thought, tastes and dispositions formed in and by those practices. The habitus takes meaning at a number of different levels: it is a metaphor for membership of a community grounded in intellectual and aesthetic considerations and is available as a key to integration into a social network of solidarity acquired in early socialization. Language is a primary quality and transmitter of habitus.
[8] See section on Indian Health Service in Chapter 2.

One of the main points of ethnography is to collect data concerning issues as participants see them. Hence, structured data collection methods were used "to control the input that triggers each participant's responses so that the output can be reliably identified" (Bernard, 1994, p. 237). Unstructured questions were a means of welcoming participants and to gather general impressions about their experiences in seeking and receiving health care and about how they felt about interacting with the health system itself. These were followed by a specified list of structured questions presented to all individuals in order to elicit their opinions about a variety of predetermined sociolinguistic topics.

Interviews, as a vehicle, give full narrative voice to individuals and their concerns. These interviews represent small convenience samplings from all ten tribes[9] of Montana on seven reservations. Additionally, daily ethnographic field notes[10] reflect thoughts and impressions during the "doing" of the interviews. Field notes also register the actual nature of the process under investigation. Segments of field notes are inserted at the end of many sections, connecting the interviewer's experiences with the interview processes.

Indigenous Methodologies

Standard academic research requires a training course and certification in Human Participants Protection Education for Research Teams, sponsored by the National Institutes of Health (NIH) and a Completion Certificate from the Institutional Review Board (IRB), which serves as protection for interactions of federal agencies, institutions, and researchers that are responsible for conducting research with human participants. Additionally, there are specific ethical and methodological considerations for conducting Indigenous research. American Indian tribes and Canadian bands are increasingly formalizing methods of research activity in their communities. In November, 1990, the United States Congress passed into law the Native American Graves Protection and Repatriation Act (NAGPRA, P.L.

---

[9] The Little Shell, though landless, includes the Métis (Chippewa and French) and is one of the largest tribes in Montana.

[10] *Writing Ethnographic Fieldnotes* (Emerson, Fretz & Shaw, 1995).

106-601) to protect American Indian material and intellectual property rights. The first formal written Indigenous research polices were established in the early 1970s by the Masset and Hesquiaht Bands in British Columbia (Nason, 1996, p. 17). In 1974, the Masset Museum and Cultural Committee adopted formal "Principles of Professional Responsibility" and also "Applications to Do Research" that require applicants to disclose all scholarly or corporate connections, sources of funding, project descriptions, publication plans, and expected royalties. All of the above requirements were followed in this study.

In 1977, the Sub-Committee of the Working Group of Canada developed "Ethical Principles to Conduct Research" that was revised in 1997 (Graham & McDonald, 1997). "Principles of the Association of Canadian Universities for Northern Studies" (ACUNS) has been the most widely cited policy adopted among researchers in Canada, although much is currently changing pertaining to land claims settlements, self-governance regulations, and more participatory collaboration in research designs and government policy. In the United States, most tribes do not yet have such formal or unified research policies in written form (Nason, 1996, p. 17). A 1996 survey of 53 American tribes and Canadian bands found that most had no formal written policies but were interested in initiating them (ibid).

Many scholars[11] addressed guidelines for ethical and methodological research regarding protocols for non-Indians who conduct research in Indigenous communities. A combination of these Indigenous methodologies was incorporated for this investigation, also informed by the "Canadian Ethical Principles for the Conduct of Research in the North" (Graham & McDonald, 1997), and Barden's (1993) comprehensive guides for best practices of Indigenous Methodology

Such principles of ethical guidelines and protocols for conducting Indigenous research require:

---

[11] Linda Tuhiwai Smith (1999), Devon Mihesuah (1998; 2004), Donald Fixico (2003), Vine Deloria, Jr., (1991b) Paul Stubbs (1993), Hilary Weaver (1997), Michael Bird (2002), and Thomas Peacock (1996).

1. Researchers to abide by any local laws, regulations or protocols that may be in place in the region(s) in which they work.

2. Appropriate community consultation at all stages of research, including design and practice. In determining the extent of "appropriate" consultation, researchers and communities should consider the relevant cross-cultural contexts and the type of research involved. However, incorporation of local research needs into research projects is encouraged.

3. Necessary respect for the language, traditions, and standards of the community and adherence to the highest standards of scholarly research.

4. Respect for the privacy and dignity of the subjects. Researchers are encouraged to familiarize themselves with the cultures and traditions of local communities.[12]

5. Research to take into account the knowledge and experience of the people and to respect that knowledge and experience in the research process. The incorporation of relevant traditional knowledge into all stages of research is encouraged.[13]

---

[12] My graduate work and research were in the fields of Native American Studies and American Studies (with a Native American focus), thus I was well versed with Indigenous methodologies and cultural and linguistic particulars of the various Montana tribes. As a non-Indian, I was an outsider by culture and followed all protocols for non-Indian research in Indian communities.

[13] This research was informed by specific tribal histories and culture. Particularly useful were Bryan, 1996; Deloria, 1998; Frantz, 1999; the setting within the cross-cultural and mainstream community (Lobo & Peters, 2001); concepts of knowledge, reality, and aspects of holistic existence (Fixico, 2003; Peat, 1994); spiritual connectedness based on harmony, balance, and respect (Beck, Walters & Francisco, 1990 [1977]; Harrod, 2000; Laduke, 1999; McCleary, 1997); knowledge that is used to help and protect the community (Cornell, 1988; Deloria & Wilkins, 1997; Waters, 2004); the importance of observing and listening to the environment (Fixico, 1998; Harrod, 2000; McCleary, 1997); the need to find rather than tell the truth (Mihesuah, 1996, 1998; Mihesuah & Wilson, 2004; Shoemaker, 2002); sources of knowledge (Bol, 1998; McCleary, 1997); to seek the Indian voice (Battiste, 2000; Thornton, 1998; Waters, 2004); what it means to live in "both worlds"—Indian and White (Battiste, 2000; Grande, 2004; Moore, 2003); the critical turns of historical issues of sovereignty (Deloria & Wilkins, 1992, 1997; Wilkens & Lomawaima, 2001); the need for better federal policies (Canby,

6. All parties to gain fully from research. Efforts should be made, where practical, to enhance local benefits that could result from research.[14]

7. The research to be accountable for all decisions on the project, including the decisions of subordinates.

8. No research involving living people or extant environments to begin before obtaining the informed consent of those who might be unreasonably affected, or the consent of their legal guardian.[15]

9. Informed consent, where researchers should clearly identify sponsors, purposes of the research, sources of financial support, and investigators responsible for the research.[16]

10. Written informed consent, where researchers explain the potential beneficial and harmful effects of the research on individuals, on the community and/or on the environment.

11. The written informed consent of participants in research involving human subjects to be obtained for any information-gathering techniques used (tape and video recordings, photographs, physiological measures, etc.) for information gathered and used from participants and for the format in which that information will be displayed or made accessible.

12. The informed written consent of participants be obtained.

1998; Carillo, 1998; O'Brien, 1989; Williams, 1997); and the need for Indians to develop "critical consciousness"—a clear awareness of reality and the need to change it—in order to realize the situation of being enslaved in current situations before becoming free (Battiste, 2000; Fixico, 2003; Grande, 2004).

[14] Guidelines of findings were provided to the central Billings IHS to distribute.

[15] Colonial and recent research interventions have too often not been disclosed and have caused traumatic collective abuses to Indians —physically, mentally, and spirituality, thus resulting in great mistrust of "outsider" research interventions. Indigenous methodologies serve to protect Indigenous communities and to be transparent in all aspects of research and to preserve cultural and intellectual property.

[16] All aspects of this research were self-funded.

13. No undue pressure to be applied to obtain consent for participation in a research project.

14. A community or individual to have the right to withdraw from the research at any point.

The interviews, flowing narratives in structure, were conducted at IHS Clinic Units and IHS Hospitals in Montana as well as at large Indian social and spiritual gatherings that included participants from all of the Montana tribes. The IHS operates the hospitals, clinic facilities, service units, as well as two tribally self-governed health facilities. These facilities were established to serve tribally enrolled Indians who qualify for federally funded services.

The IHS settings makes specific demands on health professionals' information processing and also constrains the kinds of responses that can be expressed (Gumperz & Levinson, 1996, pp. 196-197). The same holds true for patients in institutions that represent colonial power and authority.[17]

Volunteer research participants were Indian tribal members of all genders;[18] patients, students, as well as non-Indian doctors, nurses, aids, counselors, pharmacists, administrators, and staff. One of the Indian patients was also a clinician and thus had a dual means of input by "standing in both worlds." The interviews were comprised of a convenience sample.[19] Individuals were not chosen by strategies of random demographic selection, but rather on the happenstance of their presence and their willingness to take part in narrative interviews. The participants were not asked about any aspect of their socioeconomic or educational backgrounds, nor about their personal health or social beliefs, marital status, or private information. All names and identifying information were coded for confidentiality and signatures were obtained both pre- and post-interview to ensure that nothing of regret was included.

---

[17] Refer to Chapter 2.

[18] Further referenced under the heading: Confidentiality, Gossip, Gender, and Trust in Chapter 4.

[19] A convenience sample is not statistically valid, but serves to collect and identify areas that warrant further critical study.

Patients' questions about the study were freely invited and discussed. All participants were fully informed of the nature and reason for the interviews, how the results would be used, and written permission was given by each participant. This research was not funded by any outside source. Gifts (personally funded) were offered to all participants as part of tribal traditions of "gifting" to thank the volunteers who consented to be interviewed.[20]

Community collaboration was an extremely important ethical consideration for the success of this inquiry. There is an obligation to respect, spend time with, and consult with tribal leaders to collaborate in planning, gathering data, determining findings, and revealing outcomes. It is important to hear individual input, to ask for decisions and reviews, to obtain confirmation of frameworks, and to respect intellectual property rights according to NAGPRA regulations. Tribal elders, IHS unit directors, administrators, staff, community leaders, healers, and clinicians provided such input, permission, support, encouragement, and trust in me and this research.

Outcomes of research must be made available for community benefit. All too often when conducting Indigenous research, the social structures that underlie socio-political contexts are not brought forth. Mistrust based on historical misuses of research have been intrusive, abusive, inaccurate, repetitive, or useless has led to sanctioned censorship of Indigenous research. The ethical issues presented above pertain to all research done under all conditions and at all locations on Indian lands, border towns, or cities where Indian tribal members reside. Research is a complex challenge that should be approached with the highest level of awareness in any setting or culture and should benefit the tribes.

Because the focus on communications was based on the use of the English language, all of the participants had some level of English[21] proficiency, often seemingly fluent, whether as their primary or secondary language. Some of the Indian participants were raised

---

[20] Gift giving is an Indian tradition as a way of being, where cultural practices of sharing (especially food) with others and gifting at ceremonies will help keep the good spirit around (Lame Deer & Erdoes, 1972; Murray, 2000; Paper, 1988; and Weatherford, 1988).

[21] Use of English ranged from very mainstream Standard English to versions of Indian English, but all were informed by the habitus of the Indian worldview.

in their native tribal language, some learned English at school, some never had learned their tribal language, some were in the process of learning either English or their tribal language, and some were able to easily switch between languages.

An analysis of sociolinguistic findings reveals that demographics of reservation settings have a profound and widespread influence on both communication and health in relation to practices of power, kinship, respect, and time. Differences in the cultural assumptions between Indians and non-Indians inform sociolinguistic practices in both the verbal and nonverbal processes of communication, since language is both produced and received. Verbal linguistic disparities isolated in this analysis include the use of narratives, questions for gathering information, gratuitous concurrence (the tendency to agree with the questioner), politeness, silence, confidentiality, gossip, gender, and time—against a complex backdrop of power, biomedicine, demographics, and trust. Additionally, nonverbal discrepancies include eye contact, touch, modesty, proximity, and time.

This exploration is a beginning step in distinguishing communicative inequities and will be important in establishing a foundation for further research and for building a body of work to provide practical communicative training for clinicians and patients at Indian Health Care facilities and other facilities that serve Indian patients. True communication cannot be achieved unless there is considerable effort taken to lessen the separation at the often-muddled intersection where the disciplines of anthropology, linguistics, sociology, economics, and history collide and where there emerges a confluence of language and context where people encounter and express their own intensely personal lives.

As inherently difficult, if not impossible, and important as it may be to understand personal motives and actions in life, it is equally important to understand what drives the vehicles of language and to consider the context as the road upon which daily actions are navigated. Linguistic form is shaped in part by its joining to the actual situations where people express themselves, which in turn is shaped by the meaning structures of language. Questions must then be approached as to how social identity and interaction are constructed. What are the design elements of the language of verbal and nonverbal discourse that derive from and are resources for particular manners of thinking, acting, and communicating? Can language be separated from context? What happens when there is a breakdown of language in the very nature of its inherent context? When Indians seem to speak the same language as their non-Indian health providers, how do miscommunications impact them all?

These questions need to be examined through further rigorous research to reveal how they affect the chasms that are created when there is a breakdown of language and communication. This research is based on questions that are rooted in ethnographic settings with exceptionally rich and vibrant cultures, languages, and histories.

It is by understanding the workings of a language in its actual social complexity that language in general can best be understood. Because Indian reservations provide exquisite examples of any number of important facts about language and social life, they become heuristically invaluable to the study of the role of language as situated in context. Thus, this exploration proceeds from a conviction that what it tries to describe is intrinsically beneficial and worth knowing in intimate detail and is critical to the wellbeing of Indians and their clinicians.

One immediate consequence is that this examination is marked by inherent elements of empiricism, which is the first step in sketching out the approach into which it fits. There is also the matter of Indians and the unlimited number of universes this term represents, all interacting, emerging, and fully engaged in the complexities of today, just as much as in the complexities of a long past, where diversity of Indian tribes and individuals has tended to be lumped together as a single pan-Indian stereotype. It is equally obvious, if somewhat paradoxical, that these universes exist apart from scholars, yet bear their presence.

Existing health research falls into several categories. An initial category looks at the juncture where the patient and clinician intersect during the medical interview in reference to forms of communication, satisfaction, and implications for the outcomes. Since any health encounters are fraught with potential miscommunications between patient and clinician, a sociolinguistic approach is a useful tool for this investigation. Next, communications that occur among varying cultures that hold different beliefs about health will be summarized. Cultural beliefs about health are then situated in the framework of the biomedical model of Western medical practices as the encompassing nature of illness and treatment. Lastly, all forms of medical encounters, communications, health beliefs, and medical models are informed by the unconscious dispositions of experiences that are generative of individual and social structures that, in turn, also generate structure through habitus. Though these areas approach the margins of this investigation, there is no available research that specifically targets the particular question about the nature and results of sociolinguistic miscommunications that occur between Indians and non-Indians on Montana's reservation health care facilities, where both verbal and nonverbal encounters between patients and clinicians are laden with cultural assumptions.

Patient-Clinician Encounters

In reference to mainstream American culture in general, recent models of doctor-patient communications emphasize the exchange of information in promoting collaboration in the health process.[22] Observations of relationships between patient and doctor go back as far as Hippocrates ([Hippocrates], 1923), but the modern study of this field derives from the seminal work of Henderson (1935) and Parsons (1951). However, it was not until the 1960s and 1970s that particular clinician behaviors to facilitate better communication began to be methodically identified and examined by health care researchers (Bartlett, Grayson, et al., 1984). Practitioners are concerned with identifying factors that promote patient compliance with treatment directives (Buller & Buller, 1987) in order to improve the effectiveness and quality of health care.[23]

Research in the doctor-patient relationship[24] generally has studied one or more of five variables (Bartlett, Grayson, et al., 1984):

---

[22] Bartlett, Grayson, Barker, Levine, Golden & Libber, 1984; Ben-Sira, 1980; Cegala, McClure, Marinelli & Post, 2000; Street, 1991; and Thompson & Ciecbanowski, 2003.

[23] Bartlett, Grayson, et al., 1984; Korsch, Gozzi & Francis, 1968; and Lane, 1983.

[24] Robert A. Doughty has taught leadership to other physicians (interns, residents, and especially chief residents) for over four decades. He has trained over 20,000 aspiring young physicians and maintains that the essential message has remained true throughout various courses and seminars. "To maximize the effectiveness of

doctor interpersonal skills, doctor teaching skills, patient satisfaction, patient recall of instructions, and patient adherence to the regimen. Over the course of time, two principal branches of research have evolved: investigations of the effects of physician interpersonal skills as they relate to patient satisfaction and adherence to the therapeutic regimen and investigations of patient teaching and its influence on patient recall and adherence (ibid.). The latter will not be discussed in this inquiry.

Despite sophisticated technologies for medical diagnosis and treatment, conversation remains the primary means by which the doctor and patient exchange health information. The significance of information sharing in the health care consultation is readily apparent (Street, 1991). For the doctor, information is crucial for formulating diagnoses and prescribing treatment; for the patient, information fosters an understanding of one's health status, which in turn may reduce uncertainty, alleviate concerns, and improve health (Roter, Hall & Katz, 1987; Waitzkin, 1985). In addition to medical treatment, it has been found that emotional support is a latent need that patients have, and its fulfillment improves the relationship between doctor and patient as a team (Ben-Sira, 1980; Luban-Plozza, 1995).

The communication of information in reservation clinics is fraught with problems, despite acknowledged common aims of practitioners and patients. Some reasons for the problematic nature of clinical communication are incongruent cultural frames of reference about what information ought to be shared, sociolinguistic differences, and the social distance between patients and practitioners (Mathews, 1983). A model of mainstream patient-centered interactions, where the patient's point of view is actively sought by the clinician, implies that clinicians can facilitate patients' expressions to be more active and effective (Lang & Huillen, 2000; Stewart, 1984). This approach is critical to the delivery of high quality care by clinicians. However, there is considerable ambiguity concerning the

interpersonal communication, everyone (deliverer as well as recipient) must aspire to better understand the source of the recipient's reception of health communications. Creating an effective doctor-patient relationship alone is fraught with peril, but the addition of major cross cultural differences makes generating such effective relationships almost impossible."

exact meaning of the term "patient-centered care" and the most salient method of measuring its process and outcomes (Mead & Bower, 2000). This is especially problematic when situated between different cultures.

Social scientists and clinicians alike have expressed the importance of the "doctor-patient" interaction,[25] which includes issues of consumer satisfaction (Merkel, 1984), expectations of quality (Jackson, Chamberlin & Kroenke, 2001; and Kenagy, Berwick & Shore, 1999), compliance (Bartlett, Grayson, et al., 1984), power (Haug & Lavin, 1981), trust (Dibben, Morris & Lean, 2000), continuity of care (Thompson & Ciecbanowski, 2003), listening and questioning skills (Blatterbauer, Kupst & Schulman, 1976; Marvel, Epstein, Flowers & Beckman, 1999; and Stewart, 1984), and active patient participation in the health care process (Lang & Huillen, 2000; and Speedling, 1985).

Although considerable attention has been given to clinicians' information exchange over the past decades, little research has examined communication contributions from patients.[26] Research indicates that patients anywhere could benefit from training in medical communication skills in order to gain better health care from their clinicians (Cegala, McClure, et al., 2000). It has also been shown that the quality of interpersonal skills influences patient outcomes more than the quantity, and that the sum effects of communication skills on patient adherence are mediated by patient satisfaction and recall (Bartlett, Grayson, et al., 1984); aspects that would positively reduce inequities for Indian patients.

As the consumer movement continues to gain strength in health care, the concept of patient satisfaction is not merely a subtlety, but it correlates positively with variables that have a direct bearing on health and illness outcomes of morbidity and mortality (Merkel, 1984). The seminal work of Kaplan et. al. (1989) poses that the health care community has not yet exhibited a readiness to fully embrace and put into practice recommendations for improving communication

---

[25] Davis, 1968; Francis & Korsch, 1969; Garrity, 1981; Hulka, Cassel, Kupper & Burdette, 1976; Sanson-Fisher & Maguire, 1980; and Svarstad, 1999.

[26] (Anderson, 1991; Ashton, Paterniti, Collins, Gordon, O'Malley, Peterson et al., 2003; Cegala, McClure, et al., 2000; Sharf, 1988; Simons-Morton, Mullen, Mains, Tabak & Green, 1992; Webber, 1990)

The result of communicative strains and failures will later be elucidated in the context of Indian culture and health care, where dissonance in communicative skills is even wider and has a profoundly higher risk for endangering the wellbeing and life span of Indian patients who seek help in a system that does not necessarily reflect their own.

Sociolinguists and Health Care

The field of sociolinguists is an important venue for understanding how health failures occur based on the shortfalls of communication in its social context through the ethnography of speaking. An overview of sociolinguistics provides a model of language variation according to such factors as the speaker's gender, age, and social class in the broader relationship between language and society as well as the ways speakers and hearers use linguistic choices to communicate social and situational meaning. "Social networks are in turn structured by larger social forces" (Gumperz & Levinson, 1996, p. 364).

Within this broad realm of communication, sociolinguistics is the "study of the way that languages are used in social contexts" (Eades, 2003b, p. 1109) such as in the court room, the school, the job site, or the health care facility. One of the significant contributions made by sociolinguistics in understanding late 20th century society has been to uncover the role that general and specific cultural differences play in intercultural communications and miscommunications. Invaluable edited collections addressing an expansive array of topics in linguistic research are *Culture in Communication* (Di Luzio, Günthner, et al., 2001), *Intercultural Negotiation* (Rehbein, 2001), *Explorations in the Ethnography of Speaking* (Bauman & Sherzer, 1974), and *Readings in the Sociology of Language* (Fishman, 1968).

In the United States, despite sharing the basic essentials of the English language, there can be extensive differences in the interpretation of meanings and pragmatics between Indians and non-Indians (and also with other ethnicities and immigrant or marginalized cultures). The fact that Indians speak varieties of English does not mean that they share the same norms for using and interpreting it. Even when grammar and accent seem quite close, there are considerable pragmatic differences and assumptions that affect communication. "Pragmatics" is a widely used term in sociolinguistics, originally referring to "the study of speaker intentions and meaning, in contrast to semantics as the study of utterance meaning" (Eades 2003b, 1113). The term is now used quite generally to refer to the analysis of language beyond the sentence level, which always includes considerations of context, both immediate and social. Because "Indian English"[27] is a distinct rule-governed variety of English, it differs significantly from Standard English (SE)[28] in one or more of the following features: phonology, grammar, vocabulary, or pragmatics (following Eades 1995, 142). To examine meanings requires studying the relationship between the speaker and the spoken word as well as the hearer and the culture of the speakers involved.

Bringing forth subtleties of Indigenous communications, Diana Eades[29] is the foremost investigator of sociolinguistic mis/communications between Australian Aborigines who speak various degrees of fluent English and their dealings with the legal system. Her research focuses on linguistic areas of questions, narratives, seeking information, silence, eye contact, interruptions, scaffolding (structuring questions to influence the outcome), gratuitous concurrence (the habit of agreeing with a questioner for any number of reasons apart from the veracity of the proposition posed), and "verballing" (an Australian term for presenting false statements as confessions). Michael Cook (1996a; 1996b) corroborates Eades' studies with similar findings about communicative behaviors of Australian Aborigines and Indigenous New Zealanders.

Though Native Americans and Aboriginal Australians may share overlapping worldviews and linguistic experiences, there are obvious problems with grouping Indigenous Peoples together who have a variety of cultures and colonial experiences. It is necessary

---

[27] The discussion of Indian English will be expanded upon later under the heading of Indian English at the end of Chapter 2.
[28] Standard English (or SE) refers to the accepted use of the English language as a national norm in any English-speaking country, encompassing grammar, vocabulary and spelling.
[29] Eades: 1992, 1993, 1994a, 1994b, 1994c, 1995, 1996, 2000, 2002, 2003a, and 2003b.

to define "the many diverse communities, language groups and nations, each with their own identification within a single grouping" (Smith, 1999, p. 6). "Some ways of communicating that distinguish Aboriginal people from mainstream speakers of English in Australia" (Eades, 2003b, p. 1128) are also relevant in a number of intercultural and Indigenous settings in the United States.

In the realm where sociolinguistics and health care cross, Anne Fadiman (1997) in *The Spirit Catches You and You Fall Down: A Hmong Child, American Doctors, and the Collision of Two Cultures* investigates the clash between the staff of a small hospital in Merced, California, and a refugee family from Laos over the care of their Hmong daughter who is diagnosed with epilepsy. All those involved wanted what was best for Lia and her family, but the lack of understanding between them, their different languages, and their highly divergent cultures and health practices led to failures of both communication and health care. Though none of the extended Lee family or their friends spoke *any* English (in contrast to this inquiry where all of the individuals interviewed spoke some degree of English, though with different underlying concepts of Standard English and biomedical language), the traditional Hmong beliefs and practices about the causes and treatments for various interferences of health came in direct conflict with the biomedical practices of the hospitals where the Lee family sought care. Most modern biomedical facilities have no capacity to understand beliefs and practices beyond those of the typical Western biomedical mode.

In the article "Making the Biopolitical Subject: Cambodian Immigrants, Refugee Medicine and Cultural Citizenship in California," Ahiwa Ong (1995), influenced by social theorist Michel Foucault, claims that biomedicine attends to the health of bodies and is also constitutive of the social and bureaucratic practices that socialize individuals as clinicians and patients. She links the biomedical practices of the health profession to the normalization of citizenship, while expressing how Khmer refugees seek not only their traditional resources for healing but also to elude control over the body and mind that goes with Western medical care and historical practices of oppression and torture toward Cambodians.

Two other important articles relate to medical care for Indigenous populations in Ethiopia and Zimbabwe. Richard Hodes, in "Cross-cultural Medicine and Diverse Health Beliefs: Ethiopians

Abroad" (1997), illustrates how health for Ethiopians is viewed as an equilibrium between the body and the outside, where excess sun and blowing winds are causes of diseases. Most Ethiopians have faith in traditional healers and procedures, with specific cultural beliefs that are unfamiliar to and must be learned by their doctors in order to work effectively with these patients. The research in "Communication Patterns Between Health Care Providers and Their Clients at an Antenatal Clinic in Zimbabwe" (Murira, Lützen, Lindmark & Christensson, 2003) explores communications between pregnant women and health care providers at an antenatal clinic in Zimbabwe, where attitudes reflected relationships to the culture and tradition of Zimbabwe at various levels of personal or impersonal relating.

Two books that provide insight on Indian health perspectives in particular are *Medicine Ways: Disease, Health, and Survival Among Native Americans* (Trafzer & Weiner, 2001) and F. David Peat's comparison of medicines, myths, languages and the wide range of different perceptions of both Indian and non-Indian concepts of reality in *Blackfoot Physics* (1994). Excellent research specific to the usage of silence (as both practice and function) in Western Apache and Navajo tribes in this country has been conducted by Keith Basso (1970; 2001) and Margaret Montoya (2000). In addition, Susan Urmston Philips explored communicative practices on the Warm Springs Indian Reservation (1974; 1983). A critical book influencing this inquiry is William Leap's *American Indian English* (1993), where what seems to be the standard use of English is not necessarily so. All of these concepts will be fully addressed in direct relation to behaviors and treatments in the health care system.

In the field of medical anthropology (research on the cultural contexts of health, which includes roles of illness, sickness, disease, suffering, and healing), Arthur Kleinman lays the foundational research in *The Illness Narratives* (1998), *Patients and Healers in the Context of Culture* (1980), and *Writing at the Margin (1995)*. Further illuminations on these topics include *The Cultural Context of Health, Illness, and Medicine (Loustaunau & Sobo, 1997); Sickness and Healing* (Hahn, 1995); *Rethinking Illness and Disease* (Hahn, 1994); and *Physicians of Western Medicine: Anthropological Approaches to Theory and Practice* (Hahn, 1995). Though these works provide insights into traditional beliefs and practices of healing, they do not form parallel connections to linguistic practices.

These combined readings aid in highlighting the necessity of linking Indigenous sociolinguistics and health care, but none define the specific intersections of American Indian models of culture, communication, and health beliefs that occur at reservation health facilities that function in the biomedical model of Western thought and practice. This investigation strives to bridge the gulf and to provide new evidence linking the relevance of habitus in Western and biomedical practices to Indian communicative health encounters.

Biomedicine

Biomedicine is the Western practice of viewing the body as a "location" where various diseases are situated as physiological aspects that are dealt with as though they reside in a corpse-like body and are viewed by the medical gaze of the doctor who is attending the disease, dissociated from the human personality. Michel Foucault discusses how the theory illuminates the Western world of biomedicine and how it conflicts with traditional forms of non-Western concepts of health and healing. Critical theoretical contexts are provided in *The Birth of the Clinic: An Archaeology of Medical Perception (Foucault, 1984)*; *The Order of Things: An Archaeology of the Human Species* (Foucault, 1994 [1973]); "The Order of Discourse" (Foucault, 1984); *and Power/Knowledge: Selected Interviews & Other Writings* (1980).

Biomedical theory is important for understanding the construct of how mainstream Americans and clinicians relate to the body in a culturally constructed Western model. This model explains how the Indian Health Service clinicians approach Western medical treatment, but does not usually address the differing views of Indian traditions of health, healing beliefs, and practices that are situated outside of the biomedical construct.

Habitus

Habitus refers to the societal disposition, generation and inculcation of language, customs, etiquettes, interactions and behavior of the individual and how the social world is received and reacted to. Children absorb such practices as religion, nationality, ethnicity, education, relationships, and language unconsciously from their inherent cultural group and react toward the world with those built-in behaviors, individual experiences, and objective opportunities but lack knowledge that any other model exists. Group culture and personal history shape body, mind, spirit, and social action in the present. Pierre Bourdieu theorizes the creation and function of habitus. Of particular benefit are "The Economics of Linguistic Exchange (1976); "The Field of Cultural Production, or the Economic World Reversed" (1983); *Language & Symbolic Power* (1982b); and "Social Space and the Genius of Groups" (1985).

Additional useful sources addressing habitus are *Bourdieu: Critical Perspectives* (Calhoun, LiPuma & Postone, 1993)*; Culture and Power: The Sociology of Pierre Bourdieu (Swartz, 1997)*; and W.E. Hank's "Notes on Semantics in Linguistic Practice" (1993). Habitus is a complex critical tool for understanding how individuals from divergent cultures think, speak, and behave differently about the world. These are critical structural references for laying the groundwork for understanding how and why individuals in different cultures find it so difficult to comprehend the point of view of individuals from other social contexts. Habitus boldly underscores the causes for communicative and health treatment failures between cultures.

The Cornerstone

There is a scarcity of research that aims to intentionally and specifically uncover Indian habitus, health beliefs and practices, linguistic constructs, and cultural worldview and then to contrast them with mainstream Western thinking and practices in corresponding fields, which are mostly ethnocentric in view and application. There is no evident research that focuses on particular junctures of Indian habitus that encompasses social reality, identity, language and communication, and belief systems that play out in the health arena. This investigation is meant to be a cornerstone that begins to uncover innate gaps in the communicative process as relating to failures of Indian health care. It is also a call to include more Indian scholars, researchers, health professionals, and tribal members to investigate and develop communicative remedies.

The most significant practical outcome for this area of inquiry would be to engage both Indians and non-Indians (patients and clinicians) at reservation health facilities, along with tribal elders, tribal councils, IHS administrators, and community leaders to converse, to make available, and to implement specific training procedures to more effectively communicate in order to provide optimal health care services to Indian populations. This training could take the forms of written guidelines, interactive web-based training, seminars and workshops, or the designation of particular individuals to assist health clinicians arriving at reservation facilities. Training would also benefit Indians who do not understand the Euro-centric form of Standard English communication or Western biomedicine.

By linking Indian communications, health belief systems, origin stories, and colonial histories to the realm of a very different culture, it is the goal to reach better treatment and mortality/morbidity rates for the Indian population, and to seriously address the historical causes of some of the current failures in health communications and treatments. The practicality of providing better cultural and communicative training and longer commitments to IHS clinical residencies should contribute to higher patient and clinician retention rates that would allow for significant improvement in continuity and trust between Indian patients and non-Indian clinicians. Additionally, this inquiry hopes to encourage Indian students to seek further education and training in health care and communication positions in order to serve their own populations with needed understanding, harmony, respect, and trust. Some of the same barriers that interfere with Indians' entry into the health professions are parallel to communicative barriers.

Findings

The sociolinguistic themes based on the previously identified data fall into three main categories:[30] (1) the rich and complex nature of

---

[30] The practice of categorization itself belongs to the Western practice of separating and compartmentalizing natural phenomena and information into what seems an artificial compartmentalization to the Indian way of holistic thinking.

Indian reservation settings and kinship structures that strongly influence communicative patterns and health care, (2) the sociolinguistic verbal assumptions and patterns that contribute to misunderstandings, and (3) the sociolinguistic nonverbal miscommunications that cause communicative failures. The themes within and between categories are not isolated and tend to have varying amounts of overlap in usage, function, and practice as they relate to broader issues of habitus and biomedical practices.

Included in the nature of the reservation setting are demographic and socioeconomic patterns that reference abusive historical events that inform present-day health care and beliefs, the nature of life, infrastructure on the reservation, the prevailing kinship structure, the functioning of Indian Health Services (IHS), time, and the employment of clinicians.

There are crucial words, wounds, and chasms that must be interrogated and addressed for the future hope of garnering better health care and communication in Indian health care settings for both Indians and their non-Indian partners. Let this be a first step in a direction of healing.

2
THEORETICAL INTERPLAYS
OF BIOMEDICINE AND HEALTH

This investigation first examines and theorizes the rise of the Western biomedical culture and its impact on practices of the Indian Health Service. Contrasts between biomedicine and Indian health belief systems will be elucidated and related to health care on Montana's reservations, followed by an overview of the theoretical sociolinguistic framework that informs and shapes this inquiry.

The Nature and Power of Biomedicine

Before assessing the role of modern medicine as it is performed on Montana's Indian reservations (and likely many reservations in the U.S.A.), it is crucial to understand the major change that took place at the end of the 18th century and led to current medical ideology and practices. Much of what we consider as medicine today was theorized by Michel Foucault's structure of perception that highlighted how medical knowledge took on the precision previously linked only to mathematics. The body became seen as an object that could be mapped, and disease was subjected to new forms of classification. Doctors began to describe phenomena previously veiled from visibility and expression.

It will then be essential to focus on contrasts of cultural differences in the interpretations and relationships of sickness, illness, and disease across contemporary cultural boundaries. By considering the role of medicine as a subculture to the mainstream culture at large, it will be possible to look more closely at intercultural differences in assumption, practice, and belief as reflected in reservation health care in Montana.

Michel Foucault, in *The Birth of the Clinic* (1994 [1973]), demonstrated that the representations of knowledge and language follow the same profound law—a structure that underlines the theories, discourse, practices, and sensibility of a given period, insofar as they contribute to a scientific understanding of what it is to be "human." To summarize, Foucault examined practices that allow humans to treat themselves as objects in the purest sense, with the body as a corpse laid out before the doctor's gaze, and whose tangible solidarity leaves no room at all for the search for hidden significance.

Since all individuals pass through the stage of death, their elimination opens the possibility for them to be seen as objects of science. Foucault attempted to find the silent structure that sustains practices, discourse, perceptual experience (the physician's gaze), as well as knowing the subject and its objects. He then treated both reference and sense merely as phenomena. He argues that by examining language, we must suspend not only our point of view of the signified but of the signifier.

Rules governing medical discourse are related to other forces that affect medical practice, because the resulting relation of discourse to the various social, technical, institutional, and economic factors that determine medical practice are given unity. In clinical discourse, when a myriad group of relations is involved, the doctor is the sovereign, the direct questioner, the observing eye, the touching finger, the organ that deciphers signs, the integrator of descriptions, and the laboratory technician. Elaborate relations exist between the doctor's therapeutic role, pedagogic role, role as an intermediary in the dissemination of medical knowledge, and as a responsible representative of public health in the social space.

In any interpersonal encounter, power can be seen to initiate from three key sources: force, material resources, and knowledge (Toffler, 1990). Because power includes social power, or the ability to influence individuals engaged in interpersonal relationships, it presupposes the actual or perceived means to act in such an influential manner and the capacity to choose whether or not to use those means. Equality of power is not usually normative, resulting in imbalances. In Western social heritage there has been a history of male and White monopoly of social and political sources of power. The medical profession is customarily viewed as a typical example of a patriarchal system. In order for the doctor-patient[31] role to function effectively, it was found that deference to medical authority by patients was necessary (Parsons, 1951).

---

[31] When referring to biomedicine, the term "doctor" will be used to represent the defining roles of (until recent years) male power and process rather than to the general role of "clinician" generally used in other aspects of this investigation.

Traditionally, the sociological concept of the relationship between doctor and patient has been the sick role, in which the physician as practitioner is in charge, and the patient is obligated to cooperate with the physician's prescribed regimen (Haug & Lavin, 1981). More recently, this power relationship has been redefined by from a consumerist perspective, in which physician and patient bargain over the terms of the relationship. Although each brings different resources to the encounter, it is still the doctor who usually prevails as the authority.

Social control in health care manifests itself and can be analyzed at various levels—individual, social, and institutional. At the individual level, the dynamics of control are played out between clinicians—physicians, nurses, support staff—and patients, often including their family-member surrogates. Doctor-patient interaction is rooted in a power relationship; in this respect it serves as one example of a general class of professional-client relationships.

Traditional sociological theory regarding professionals, awards power to doctors based on the command of an esoteric body of knowledge, acquired through academic training and leavened by service orientations toward the client. This model of professional power over clients has been incorporated in the central concept of medical sociology: the sick role. Viewing the ill person as deviant and the medical practitioner as an agent of social control (Parsons, 1951) implies this power relationship. Indeed, the obligation of the sick to seek expert help in order to get well explicitly involves deferring to professional authority in receiving and accepting information and instructions on how to end a deviant status (Coe, 1970).

The modern individual, as objectified, analyzed, and fixed is an historical accomplishment. There is no universal person on whom power has performed its functions, knowledge, and inquiries. Rather, the individual is the effect and object of certain intersections of power and knowledge—the product of complex strategic developments in the field of power and the multiple developments in human sciences. Power is not a commodity, a position, a prize, or a plot; it is the habitus operation of the political technologies throughout the social body. The functioning of these political rites of power is exactly what sets off unequal and asymmetrical relations such as seen in both "mainstream" and reservation clinics. Although relationships of power are imminent to institutions, power and institutions are not identical. The larger the difference in culture and language, the greater the realm of dominant power.

Authority is classically defined as the right to influence and direct behavior, such right having been accepted as valid and legitimate by others in the relationship (Haug & Lavin, 1981). In the medical context, authority is defined as the patient's grant of legitimacy to the physician's exercise of power, on the assumption that it will be benevolent. The relationship is asymmetrical: The patient is in a dependent position and the doctor holds a superordinate, position (Suchman, 1965).

Although the degree of dependence may vary by the patient's health condition (Szasz & Hollender, 1956), social status (Arluke, Kennedy & Kessler, 1979), or ethnicity (Segall, 1976), both parties supposedly accept this asymmetry as appropriate and desirable. It is the knowledge of the "competence gap" between doctor and patient that justifies both the professional's assumption of the authority and the client's trust, confidence, and norm of obedience (Parsons, 1975). A consumerist stance, then, clearly constitutes a challenge to physician authority.

Thus, a doctor's power and knowledge are not separate. They have functioned mutually throughout history. Neither can be explained by the other, nor reduced to the other. Power and knowledge directly imply one another, for there is no power relation without the correlative establishment of a field of knowledge, nor any knowledge that does not simultaneously presuppose and constitute power relations. Power needs knowledge of practice to operate, and only through encounters with practice can practice be known.

The hospital became the physical counterpart of the medical discipline and was neither benign, insignificant, nor inconsequential. The importance of the examination in the hospital setting or other health care institutions is based on a subtle but important reversal, where traditional forms of power are made visible, put in the open, and on constant display to be witnessed through the medical gaze. Patients are thus kept in the dark, illuminated only slightly at the margins by the light of power. Disciplinary power, however, reversed these relations.

Power itself sought invisibility, and the object of power—those on whom it affects—was made most visible. It was this fact of observation and constant visibility (gaze) that was the key to disciplinary technology. In this locale of domination, disciplinary power manifested its potency by arranging "objects." The examination became the object of the ritual of this objectification. It is through this reversal of visibility that power now maneuvers in the medical setting.

Patients need power to have their health needs met and to meet their own responsibilities. They need to present both factual (biomedical) and narrative (psychosocial) aspects of their story in each interaction when considering the ethical use of power (Goodyear-Smith, Buetow & Buetow, 2001, p. 453).

Sources of Power in the Doctor-Patient Relationship[32]

Type of power	Doctor's source of power	Patient's source of power
Legal and social authority or *"Muscle"*	Social authority and status	Social standing and legal rights
Material wealth or *"Money"*	Available medical resources and high compensation	Financial resources to pay for medical care (including insurance or subsidy)
Information and knowledge exchange or *"Mind"*	Medical knowledge and skills	Self-knowledge; beliefs and values about one's own health problems

Power can be used or misused in doctor-patient relationships. Who uses power and its intent must be considered in assessing whether it is used positively or negatively.

---

[32] Based on (Goodyear-Smith, Buetow, et al., 2001, p. 451).

Examples of the Misuse of Power in the Doctor-Patient Relationship:[33]

Type of power	Misuse by doctor	Misuse by patient
Social authority	"Playing God," e.g. using selective euthanasia, genome manipulation, or abortion to create an improved human population.	Using high social standing to obtain unfair access to medical resources e.g. by-passing the waiting-list line.
Material resources	Making decisions about investigative or management resources influenced by one's own monetary gain.	Failing to pay for services received (excluding cases of genuine poverty); Engaging in unscrupulous lawsuits against doctors for the primary motive of making money.
Information & knowledge	Withholding medical information from the patient to maintain a position of superiority; Continuing treatment when the doctor's knowledge and skills are inadequate;	Withholding information (e.g. denying or minimizing alcohol, drug, or tobacco use); Providing the doctor with misinformation (e.g. falsely claiming compliance with the doctor's treatment); Consciously or unconsciously manipulating the doctor to initiate examinations, investigations, or treatments that the doctor may regret upon reflection.

---

[33] Based on Goodyear-Smith, Buetow, et al., 2001, p. 454.

	Controlling or punishing a patient because the patient is not following advice or is disliked; Making decisions not in the patient's best interest, based on the doctor's own beliefs and values.	Sabotaging the doctor's attempts at diagnosis and treatment.

Contradictions or complexities may arise when doctors and patients disagree. A doctor might focus on the medical treatment of a disease, whereas the patient's main task might be to find the personal meaning of the condition and its management by telling a narrative,[34] for example. A tension may also arise when the health needs of patients and the capacity of the health care system's resources to meet those needs are scarce. Under the best of circumstances, it is not always possible to empower all individuals in an interaction, especially when compromise is needed.

The status of who holds power and how it is exercised will vary among cases, but when each party considers and acknowledges the inherent power issues, more opportunities for success will ensue. Indians "were not benefiting equally from the cumulative scientific knowledge and advanced medical capacity to diagnose, treat and cure disease" (Mayberry, Mili & Ofili, 2000, p. 109), again highlighting an asymmetry of power in the health care system, especially as it applies to marginalized communities or particularly relating to rural Montana reservation settings for health care.

---

[34] The topic of narratives will be discussed in Chapter 4, under the heading of Verbal Miscommunications.

Indian Health Service

Indians in Montana who live on reservations or are tribal members have access to health facilities and health care that is provided by the Indian Health Service (IHS) (Matiella, 1994, p. 281). The governmental duty to provide health services to Indian tribes derives from many sources, including negotiated treaties to ceded Indian lands, settlements, agreements, and legislation. Significantly, there are specific treaties signed by the federal government and Indian tribes, exchanging Indian land and resources for federal promises of health care and other services. While this obligation is widely accepted, it has not been upheld by the court as a basis for Indian legal entitlement to benefits. Thus, responsibility for Indian health care as recognized by Congress has been subject to judicial and administrative disavowal at the expense of Indians, further serving to reinforce institutional power that attacks Indian sovereignty.

National IHS provides health care services to approximately 1.43 million Indians living on reservations, in rural communities, and in urban areas. The IHS care system consists of health centers, hospitals, and health stations that are managed by 144 service units and 11 Area Offices. IHS services are delivered in three ways: through direct IHS services; through tribal services; or by contract with non-IHS service providers.

At the time of this inquiry, the annual appropriation for IHS is approximately $5.5 billion. The amount and effectiveness of the appropriations varies with frequent changes in the Indian Healthcare Improvement Act (IHCIA) legislation. Appropriations are made based on the assumption that IHS health care will be provided in combination with public programs such as Medicare and Medicaid, for which Indians qualify as United States and sovereign state citizens. However, access to public programs by Indians is often denied or delayed, based on the erroneous belief that Indians are only entitled to IHS health care. Additionally, the erratic funding of the IHCIA has made it very difficult for the IHS to fulfill its goals of providing the best care necessary to achieve the "highest health status possible."

The Billings Area Indian Health Service (Billings Area IHS, n.d.) that serves Montana provides services to approximately 60,021

Indians living in Montana and Wyoming. The average age of this population is 22.3 years with 67.6 percent of the people having a high school diploma or higher. Seven of the eight service units are located in the State of Montana: Blackfeet, Crow, Flathead, Fort Belknap, Fort Peck, and Northern Cheyenne. The Confederated Salish and Kootenai Tribes and the Rocky Boy service unit have compacted under self-governance. The eighth unit is in Wyoming.

Many of the health problems encountered on a daily basis may be traced to poor socioeconomic conditions that contribute to unemployment and inadequate housing. Most of the health services delivered in IHS clinics address accidents, prenatal care, diabetes, hypertension, and respiratory infections. The emphasis on health promotion and disease prevention activities nationwide has led to the development of reservation-based Community Fitness Centers. At least one such program has been started on each reservation in Montana, and the centers are well utilized.

IHS units and tribal self-governance facilities provide ambulatory, emergency, dental, environmental and community health, and preventive health services through their hospitals and clinics. Medical services that cannot be treated at these facilities are provided through contractual arrangements with physicians and hospitals in various outlying communities. Three of the service units—Blackfeet, Crow, and Fort Belknap—have hospitals that provide both inpatient and outpatient care. The staffing breakdown in the Billings area consists of approximately 47.3 percent professional staff and approximately 52.6 percent ancillary staff. A number of direct care health, preventive, and community health services elevate the health status of the Billings-area Indian population. These services are provided through health educators, public health nutritionists, school mental health programs, public health nurses, community health representatives, coordination of care, and special projects and initiatives.

In addition to medical care provided in IHS facilities, specialty services/care are purchased from the private sector through the Contract Health Services program (CHS). The purpose of the CHS program is to provide health services otherwise not available to patients in IHS facilities, either because the illness is beyond the capacity of the IHS program or because the patient is temporarily away from the IHS delivery area. Referral sources are established with specialty care providers/facilities for patients who meet the specific CHS eligibility requirements and need specialty care.

It should also be well understood that few IHS clinicians are Indian. A growing number of physician assistants and nurses are Indian, however. Most Indians are quite aware that many physicians are contracted to practice at IHS facilities for a year or two after medical school to fulfill obligations to defer medical school loans. Other physicians are employed for temporary or intermittent care when needed to supplement IHS and CHS staffing needs. Indian patients commonly refer to such temporary physicians as "rent-a-docs." This system of rapid turnover of physicians may well suit physicians' financial situations and fulfill the need for physician services at IHS facilities, but it also has a direct and negative impact on Indian patients who experience a lack in the building of personal bonds, commitment, concern, continuity of care, trust, and cultural and communicative competence.

Indians perceive physicians who practice for a short term with financial motives, rather than by personal choice, as often failing to take initiatives to understand or appreciate the reservation setting. Indian patients clearly perceive them as taking the easy way out: getting an easy paycheck for work that is easier than if they had their own practices, avoiding personal connections, and whining about expectations that are seen as too easy to begin with. Indian patients often experience this program as insulting and a poor remedy for adding staff members, as this narrative illustrates:

> *I think they look at it as an easy paycheck. It's a hospital where they can probably get away with things, they make a good amount of money and they look at those two things and think, okay, well I can stay here and deal with these people. I know for a fact that the doctor I'm talking about does not have any type of relationship with the people. He don't live in the community, he lives outside of the community. You never see him in the restaurant, you never see him in the stores. It's just like he goes to work, goes home. I think before they send any doctor to a reservation to do their internships, they should let them know a lot more about the community, about the people, about traditions. So I guess when you have a new doctor in, I think it would probably take a little bit*

more time, because you're walking in the hospital and the first time you're used to seeing certain faces of certain doctors, and then you got a new doctor there. It's going to be a little uncomfortable. —David (Indian patient)

Clinical classifications of Indian diseases include Type 2 diabetes, cancer, depression, suicide, stress, violence, and substance abuse (Hodgkinson, 1990). According to the Billings statistics (Billings Area IHS, n.d.), the leading causes of outpatient visits in the Billings area are diabetes, acute otitis media, upper respiratory infections/common cold, hypertensive disease, pharyngitis, influenza, and tonsillitis/non-strep infections. Some of the leading causes of direct inpatient visits are pneumonia, alcoholic psychoses, liver disease, alcohol dependence syndrome, complications of childbirth delivery, and asthma. Some of the leading causes of contract inpatient visits are fractures, gallbladder, pneumonia, and respiratory complications of diabetes. The above causes for care are overall for all service units; however, diabetes mellitus, acute otitis media, and hypertensive diseases are a prevalent problem for all service units and are among the top ten causes for visits.

The leading causes of death in the Billings area from 1989 through 1991 were heart disease, accidents and their adverse effects, cancer, chronic liver disease and cirrhosis, and diabetes. The leading causes of infant deaths during the same time period were Sudden Infant Death Syndrome (SIDS), congenital anomalies, accidents, and perinatal infections.

Health and Belief Systems

Patients and healers are basic components of both traditional and biomedical systems and thus are embedded in specific configurations of cultural meanings and social relationships (Kleinman, 1980, pp. 24-25). They cannot be understood apart from this relationship. Illness and healing are also part of the system of Indian health care. Within that system, they are articulated as culturally constituted experiences and activities, respectively. In the context of culture, the study of patients and healers (and illness and disease) must, therefore, start with an analysis of health care and various belief systems.

When cross-cultural studies focus on disease, patients, practitioners, or healing, without locating them in particular health care systems, they seriously distort social reality.

If all of these factors come into play, how might the definition of "health" actually be pinpointed? Medical anthropologists, historians, sociologists, and health policy administrators tend to define health as a contrast to or in reference to illness.[35] The World Health Organization (WHO) declares health to be "a state of complete physical, mental, and social well-being and not merely the absence of disease or infirmity."[36]

In many Indian cultures, however, health (or "wellness") can be expressed as a balance between body, mind, and spirit or soul[37] with moral ways of knowing and enacting this balance.[38] Interactions among people and natural elements also influence health, with the assistance of beings, healers and shamans of the natural world. "[I]deas about health are founded in Indian oral narratives as well as historical and cosmological teaching that are shaped within sociocultural contexts" (Trafzer & Weiner, 2001, p. viii). All peoples were in a state of health during primordial times, according to oral narratives.

> *I don't think folks here, and that probably includes me, think about their bodies as separate entities to be operated upon one way or the other. Well, the body [is not] separate from the spirit, separate from the heart, separate from. . . . All of me is attached, I don't have a dualistic universe, and that's kind of different because it may even mean I have different priorities about how I want to deal with something.*
> —Teresa (non-Indian)

---

[35] Doyal & Pennell, 1979; Hahn, 1995; Kleinman, 1973a, 1973b, 1980, 1995, and 1998.

[36] The preamble to the Constitution of the World Health Organization (WHO) as adopted by the International Health Conference, New York, 19-22 June, 1946; signed on 22 July 1946 by the representatives of 61 states (Official Records of the World Health Organization, no. 2, p. 100) and entered into force on 7 April 1948.

[37] An outstanding description of health and wellness can be found in John Molina (see References Cited).

[38] Barden, Boyer, et al., 1993; Deloria, 1991a; Goulet, 1998; and Kawagley, 1995.

Traditional oral narratives illustrate how illness and health of one or more of the first beings were caused by jealousy, treachery, or unwise use of power. As in times past, there is a transfer of life between beings for nourishment of the body or soul. Indian cultural ideas of health, illness, and mortality are represented by both positive and negative powers that are in jeopardy today due to disturbances of the integration of the body with secular social connections.[39] For days, months, years, or generations following, disharmony may result and be considered to disrupted sacred or secular ties, which can be overlooked as a physical illness.

Inherently linked to biomedicine, disease is usually described by health clinicians as purportedly objective, decontextualized (Nadar, 1996), and measured by physical change in the structure or functioning of the body (Helman, 1995, 2000, p. 44). Because ethnicity and socioeconomic position in the United States are so closely related, they are contextualized as a powerful determinant of disease and primary health care use. They act through the agents of poorer housing and nutrition, lower education and economic opportunity, greater environmental risks, and lower socioeconomic position to cause poorer health and shortened survival.[40]

Historical health concerns regarding Indians focused on biomedically identified infectious conditions such as typhoid, diphtheria, respiratory ailments, measles, smallpox, tuberculosis, syphilis, and trachoma. Problems self-identified by Indians included fevers and sickness of mysterious origins, sorcery, forced migration from ancestral homelands, and spiritual beings. Collective colonial emotional torment, hunger, and the deterioration of tribal environmental, economic, social, and political resources all contributed to these dilemmas. Other specific social injuries include forced assimilation, boarding schools, and colonial annihilation.

In contrast, (Trafzer & Weiner, 2001, p. ix-x) histories of suffering that influence contemporary constructions of, beliefs about, and strategies to prevent, detect, and treat health problems include

---

[39] Many accidents or injuries, for example, may be traced to social and/or religious violations. Indians may see that a child might break an arm due to the visible and causal jumping from a tree, or it may be due to improper social behavior of the child or its kin.

[40] Lantz, House & Pepkowski, 1998; and Sorlie, Backlund & Keller, 1995.

alarming current health concerns, traceable to local and national histories and policies. A contemporary indigenously defined illness is a loss of power accompanied by pain and weakness that may be associated with the preceding lists of clinical conditions.[41] The symptoms that accompany collective loss of power extend to the entire community.

The healing strength of Indians in some regions may also be negatively influenced by the loss over time of multitudes of healers and shamans whose declined population has diminished the ability to protect people over the decades (Trafzer & Weiner, 2001, p. x). The loss of such leaders is noted:

> *You've got elders who are dying off, and those influential figures are not in the community.* —Alan (Indian patient)

Fortunately, Indians and tribes are not fatalistic or passive but tend to take action to rectify ailments by making use of a multiplicity of health care systems, often employing two or more distinct structures of health. Making a choice can be a complex decision-making process, especially for those in ill health, and choices may be linked to cultural acceptability, economic and infrastructural access, and efficacy.

Political structures also have a large impact on utilization of health care as well as health status.[42] These phenomena are not unique to Indians, but are common throughout the world.[43] They are particularly acute in Indian health strategies because of the pervasive domination of Euro-American governments upon Indian communities and their status as sovereign nations. The health-seeking process is not always sequential: a person may forego care, then seek

---

[41] Farmer, 2003; Hodgkinson, 1990; and Trafzer & Weiner, 2001.

[42] These issues are discussed in Trafzelr and Weiner's *Medicine Ways: Disease, Health, and Survival Among Native Americans,* Walnut Creek, CA: AltaMira Press.

[43] See Scrimshaw, S. (1992). Adaptation of anthropological methodologies apply to rapid assessment of nutrition and primary health care. In N. S. Scrimshaw & G. R. Gleason (Eds.), *Rapid assessment producers: Wualitative methodologies for planning and evaluation of health-related programmes*). Boston: International Nutrition Foundation for Developing Countries.

preventative measure, episodic care, and later use two or three systems of care (Chrisman, 1977, p. 351-78). This clinician explains his frustration with his comprehension of episodic care rather than long-term preventative care and feels that Indian patients don't make their health a priority aligned with a biomedical model:

> *You see the people that want episodic care. They don't want continuity. If you talk to them about their health, they just want to get something taken care of and no effort or mindfulness on their own part and no intention or any interest in hearing about health promotion, health care, what they can do to prevent things, how they can take care of problems next time. They just want to be given something— a quick fix. And that has nothing to do with whatever they were doing or make any changes in their lifestyle. It's really frustrating. I've come to that conclusion. I've talked to other people and that's what they see in their practice. It's just in and out. Just give them the necessary antibiotics, whatever, don't do things, don't follow up, don't look at the chart because if you talk to people who aren't interested in their health care, all it does is make them angry—they sit there looking at their watch, they want to leave, they sit there and aren't interested, and they get offended, and it makes for a lot of discord in medicine, unless you've lost your idealism or you're being selective and maybe someone comes in who actually does care about it. It create just episodic care and it doesn't enhance taking care of long-term problems like diabetes and blood pressure, things like that.* —Ken (non-Indian clinician)[44]

Familiarity with specific cultural expectations of health and healers is valuable as well as the sociolinguistic approaches differing cultures have toward the topic of health and healing. Reservation physicians should become familiar with traditional healing practices and acknowledge that Western ways of medicine aren't the only ways, especially on reservations or other marginalized communities

_____

[44] Forthcoming Indian narratives in later chapters offer differing interpretations about the nature of such visits with doctors who see patients in a different light.

that range from rural to inner city. Through an interdisciplinary approach, "ideas, methods, problem-frames from social science, and clinical science" (Kleinman, 1980, p. xi) should be considered. Traditional Indian beliefs about illness and death are described through stages of life:

I'm going to be [in my 60s] and I grew up [on this reservation] and very few White people. So I'm just a real, very traditional [person] and what they believe in that everything is very parallel. What they consider bad, bad health or what they consider good, good health and all that, parallels what is acceptable medical belief. So there is nothing really weird about this culture. In fact, what they believe in, like the grief process. They go through that, it's very similar to what, you know death and dying, the grief thing. They believe in life and they fear death. They believe in letting go, but they also know that it takes time to heal, to go through the stages of life. —Emilie (Indian patient)

Though doctors need to establish a good rapport with their patients, they also need to understand tribal origins and cultural backgrounds. Any barrier to this understanding can negatively affect doctor-patient relationships and hinder treatment. There needs to be awareness of such issues as "racism, different health-belief systems, different diagnostic possibilities, as well as a special sensitivity towards the illness" (Fuller & Toon, 1988, p. 1).

Experts in medical anthropology and cross-cultural medicine use questions designed to elicit a patient's "explanatory" model of how they experience their health and illness. These questions are meant to bypass the typical biomedical model of questioning in order to determine the health beliefs from patients from minority or immigrant cultures. Questions such as those listed below (Fadiman, 1997), based on Kleinman's work, would be beneficial to non-Indian clinicians in drawing out Indian patients' beliefs and concerns about the illnesses that bring them to reservations health facilities:

1. What do you call the problem?
2. What do you think has caused the problem?
3. Why do you think it started when it did?

4. What do you think the sickness does? How does it work?
5. How severe is the sickness? Will it have a short or long course?
6. What kind of treatment do you think you should receive? What are the most important results you hope to receive from treatment?
7. What are the chief problems the sickness has caused?
8. What do you fear most about the sickness?

Clinicians must be able to be aware of the culture and background of the patient by seeking answers to questions like these and be able to speak across the cultural and linguistic divide in order to provide treatments that fit the illnesses. Non-Indian clinicians must try to break through the tenets of biomedicine in order to meet their patients' needs, regardless of their awareness of their own impeding determinants of culture or racism. Indian patients clearly express knowledge of their perceived low status and lack of control in the dominant society.

Concurrent dual ethnocentrism is a component of every health care relationship where health care professionals are assessing, judging, evaluating, and reacting to clients on the basis of their own cultural values, medio-centric points of view, and expectations. Simultaneously, clients are using their cultural values to judge and evaluate health care providers and the Western health care system. According to Lydia DeSantis (1994), some of these concepts make health care clinicians highly aware that everyone in the clinical setting functions under the influence of personal cultural rules, some that are shared and some that are not. Two Indian patients describe how they believe clinicians view the Indian culture:

> They [doctors who take reservation jobs to help defray their loans, or "rent-a-docs"] come here with the attitude of a person that, well, I'm going to go here and provide services to these poor ignorant Indians. They come here thinking, they should be somewhere else, they're looking down instead of, you know. They're looking down on the Natives and they're thinking that they're better than this, they should

be in a better location, a better paying job, seeing patients of a better class. —Russell (Indian)

One [doctor] came about two to three years ago and he thought we were Aborigines, like the Australian Aborigines, the same thing. He thought we were the same thing. I think he thought we were practically Black. —Karen (Indian patient)

Critical medical anthropologists [45] and followers of Marx, Engles, Virchow, and Parsons may stress that notions of health reflect issues of economic productivity, shaped by ideological and social relations of political and economic structures of production and exploration (Navarro, 1985; Waitzkin, 1986).

Illness and sickness occur partly because of the colonial destruction and manipulation of Indian sociocultural, economic, and political environments. Illness and sickness are also steeped in personal and collective harms and blame. Individuals and communities are perceived to be at least partially responsible for their own health, a condition that also includes interactions of social, intellectual, spiritual essences, symbols, and metaphors of existence as a community (Becker, 1997; Scheper-Hughes & Lock, 1987). Judgment and blame from clinicians is seen by the following patient as undermining the efforts of patients to struggle with their health problems:

Racial issues and poverty issues, they work a couple of ways. They create an unequal playing field and that happens internal to both parties. People who are not suffering don't necessarily understand. I think, particularly in this country, there's that underlying puritanical thing that says: if I have, it's because I deserve. And if you don't, it's because it's your fault. And you're going to say, well most people are more sympathetic than that. Well they are, but that doesn't affect their need to feel justified in being who they are. You can't

---

[45] Baer & Singer, 1986; Eisenberg & Kleinman, 1981; Frankenberg, 1980; Kleinman, 1973a, 1973b, 1974, 1980, 1995, 1998; Kleinman, Das & Lock, 1996; Kleinman, Eisenberg & Good, 1978; Kleinman & Sung, 1979; and Singer, 1986, 1989.

*walk around having guilty feelings because you have a de-
cent car or something so you decide that you deserve that
car. But the corollary of that goes unspoken, which is that if
I deserve it, well you don't, if you don't have it. I don't know
how you get out of that frame of reference because it's there
for everybody. It works the other way too. Well, and underneath it, too, there are messages that are given to you that if
you're ill, it's your fault too. Like for example, this may be
interesting to you, too, and I'm perfectly willing to admit it,
but I weighed over 300 pounds in February. It'll be two
years since I decided that I would tackle that issue. It was a
very difficult issue to tackle because the assumption was, of
course, it was my fault that I was that way. We don't mean
to do that to each other, but we do it, and so if you have a
problem, well you brought it on yourself. We think that
about alcoholics, any kind of addiction, we think that about
[you're weak]. And not only that, willfully so, you choose or
you didn't choose, but one way or the other it's volitional,
and I think that's very hard on people because that means
you're being judged in your own mind as well as somebody
else's and the judgment you have to live with then is your
own. And to get out of that is a very, very hard thing to do.
And people who are supposed to be your helpers who are
carrying those judgments as well, are thereby invalidated as
helpers. How are they going to help somebody when they're
sitting in judgment on them? I don't know how you get out
of that. It's very difficult. So you really do have to remove
yourself from the judgment to begin to address the issue.
That's a tough thing to do.* —Teresa (non-Indian)

The possibility of increasing behavior change, especially in such
areas as weight loss, exercise, diet, drinking, smoking, and drugs is
an important link with improved disease outcomes (Lang & Huillen,
2000), especially in Indian communities where these outcomes apply to the high rates of obesity and diabetes. Complying with clinicians' directives is significant as communicative outcomes and compliance cooperation regarding personal and health concerns that
builds upon the satisfaction component, and most importantly, contributes to better health conditions for the individual, family, and

community. These clinicians relate their efforts and struggles in trying to help patients follow directives for improving their health, which is a dilemma for both clinicians and their patients. These non-Indian clinicians clearly see that disease exists in a social context:

I actually have techniques to find out what they really know versus, for instance, I have done a lot of work just seeing what patients think raises their blood sugar. I can ask them one simple question when I'm in the clinic because I only have a short amount of time to work with them. I can ask them what do you believe raises your blood sugar the most? I can really tell just by one question what their comprehension is. And I do it with other things too, people with high blood pressure, overweight, and things like that. Well, I guess the compliance thing, that is variable in every population I've ever worked with. I have gotten to the point where I work it out in small steps. And I give them several options of small steps. I was trying to get somebody to move more, she drove here, backed her car out her driveway to the mailbox. Her first goal was to walk to the end of the driveway, get her mail and walk back to her car. So I mean, I give them a lot of suggestions and then I ask them, what do you think you can do, what would you like to work on for next week? And then, believe it or not, or next month or whenever I'm seeing them again, I would say, I have maybe half of them who are willing to do it. If they're coming in the door, if they're coming back, even if they've done nothing, they're going to talk about something and maybe get some new strategies to help them. Half the battle is getting them to come back. And to understand that if they're not able to manage something, they're not going to be blamed, there's not going to be a lot of blame, why couldn't you do this?

Understand that's just my approach, but I do still see sometimes the physicians do see a lot of people who are not complying, aren't taking their medicines, aren't checking their blood sugars, continue to smoke after their heart attacks, and things, and they get very frustrated. And it is easy to say, well, why can't they just do this? But I think the thing I see the most difference here is the socio[economic], the psychological social issues that are going on. There's a lot of unemployment, there's a lot of substance abuse, not that that isn't everywhere. There's all these family issues, they may not have enough food to eat or somebody else is using it for other things. They might have children that are in trouble, and I see a lot of that—I'm thinking maybe higher than off the reservation. So these people are worried more about how am I going to have food for supper tonight? How am I going to get a ride even to the clinic, because my car's not running? Stuff like that. —Paula (non-Indian clinician)

In spite of all our teaching and emphasis and urging and cajoling and pleading to get them to follow their diets, they don't. To get them to exercise, they won't. A few are great success stories, those that do as we ask them, do get it under good control and some of them come off their medications altogether, because they have their diabetes totally under control with exercise and diet. The vast majority of them don't. They just barely get it under control and there's a goodly number, probably a quarter of them, that just can't seem to get control. They don't want to. Either they can't [change], because they don't have the money to pay for real food or they have things like some of them do, they're just massively overweight and it hurts to exercise so they don't. Those are two things if they could exercise and watch their diet, they wouldn't have diabetes. —Evan (non-Indian clinician)

I think a lot of diabetics they do take their meds. It may be naïve of me, but I really think there's a lot that do. I know a nurse that's diabetic and she's like, I've got to do something because her blood sugar's almost 300. She goes, I just can't quit sitting and eating. And if I get antibiotics I can't say that I always take my antibiotics like I'm supposed to, so how can you expect a sick person to take their medicine like they're supposed to? —Lynn (non-Indian clinician)

Most reservations do not have supermarkets or fresh produce and healthy foods, but must rely on mini-markets and fast food, leaving residents at risk for diabetes and other diseases related to food intake. Additionally, one aspect of compliance is how well the patient understands the dietary instructions given by the clinician. Most Indian patients expressed that they dislike hearing medical terms because they don't understand them and prefer lay terms and explanations so that they can follow directives:

> *I think anybody would appreciate the everyday language and not maybe use the medical term, but describe it in language that most people can understand. I think that's the best way to do that. Then people have a better understanding of what exactly is wrong with them.* —David (Indian patient)

> *They usually talk a little bit more medical terminology and, if you ask them a question, they almost repeat the same thing they said in the first place. Then you have to ask, "Can you just please explain it in layman terms?" When how many really know medical terminology? We're there 'cause we think we have a problem or illness, so we like them to explain it to us. They may explain it in medical terminology, whatever it may be. I don't know, understand it half the time.* —Vine (Indian patient)

> *Just like when you're trying to explain your symptoms, and like they just kind of seem to accept them fast, like they already know what you're talking about and stuff and maybe take and get the whole description out, and then when they explain to you what's going on, they can sometimes use big words. Like words you don't really know what they're talking about. Sometimes I ask 'em, and many times I just like I read on the Internet a lot, 'cause there's a lot of information on the Internet, so like I can always look up stuff on the Internet, too.* —Carla (Indian patient)

Many Indians perceive that more of the nurses than doctors seem generally aware of the patients' need to hear information in words they are comfortable with and are sensitive enough to patients' sense of status. They feel that it is often the nurses who fill in information that the patient feels is not obtained from the physician:

I think it depends on what their comprehension level is. I always give it to them in lay terms, but if I'm giving the handout for instance, I tell them the exact terms, I tell them their exact lab values and what they should be, because I think some people talk down to them and tell them, they say, "Well I've had diabetes for ten years, why didn't any of them, and I have many of them, when I come into there, why didn't somebody tell me that before?" And they feel insulted if you talk down to them, so you need to make a pretty rapid assessment of where they're at, unless somebody already knows them and can tell you that, because they will be insulted if you do talk down to them. —Paula (non-Indian clinician)

You've got to talk in lay terms to them, such as "prenatals." You don't ask them if they've got edema but you ask them if they've got swelling of the hands or feet. —Lynn (non-Indian clinician)

If you have a disorder or disease or something, give them the Internet site or give them someone in the community that they can go talk to about that problem. Or, have somebody on staff that they can go and have that explained to them. Or just simply explain it to them when you tell them what they got. Truthfully, a five-minute interview. Here's what you have, here's what I see, here's what you need to do, I know you can do it. A lot more of that needs to be done. —Emilie (Indian patient)

A pervasive theme for Indian patients is that they want to be treated as human beings and not as minority underdogs who deserve little attention or respect. Indian patients feel as though they are less than humans when they enter Indian health facilities:

I went to IHS, and I was seen by a physician's assistant. He was a Native American. I was so like relieved, and it felt so good to be seen by him, because he just treated me with respect, you know, like a human being, like I was worth-while, like my time and my illness at that time was important to him, and he wanted to treat it, and it was just like a breath of fresh air. It was like, um, it was so nice. —Brigette (Indian patient)

I think it has to do with the fact that hospitals is very impersonal places and patients aren't given the human dignity that they deserve as a human being, rather they're just kind of seen as a customer or, you know, a patient. And so, yeah, I think that one of the things I've always felt a lot of is that a lot of the doctors I've dealt with don't really seem to care about their patients in a human way. You know, they kind of have a "let's get down to business" attitude. —Alan (Indian patient)

Because they just kind of rush you through, like, I don't know. Sometimes I wonder like if they see you as a person or just as like, I mean as a person, like really with a problem, or just like try to get your questions answered as fast as possible and just, like more like the symptoms or something. —Carla (Indian patient)

Oh there's a lot of times an alcoholic comes in and they're treated like dirt. They're, umm, when we get them on the ambulance we treat them like human beings because we're related to people here and they're our family and we always treat people like human beings and not like they're beneath us, and a doctor will see an alcoholic come in and make comments about them and make judgments. Yeah, they make terrible comments rather than treatments, It's like, here comes so and so again, and we've had them come in, in really bad shape, we've had some of them die, they've been so bad, because they do get to the point where they die, but they're still human beings and they're still our family, they shouldn't be treated that way, they should be treated like anybody else. —Jackie (Indian patient/clinician)

It is important to note that health beliefs often rely on smudging as a critical element of the traditional healing ritual. Smudging serves to cleanse the mind, body, and spirit. Sacred herbs are burned to produce a smoke cloud that is used in various cleansing or prayer ceremonies for purification and for healing rituals. A healer, shaman, or medicine man fans the smoke over the ill person. Sacred smudging materials include herbs such as Indian tobacco, sweet grass, sage and cedar or juniper that are burned as part of a healing ritual or ceremony. It is the smudging that often initiates the healing process. In some instances, smudging enhances sensitivity or alters the state of consciousness, enabling the healer to assess and treat the illness. The smoke is thought to disperse impurities, send prayers to rise to the Spirit World, and allow negative thoughts and emotions to be lifted away. This important ritual is often not in compliance with clinic or hospital fire codes. Great efforts have been made to provide smudging areas where healers may perform this traditional ritual of healing and to allow shamans, medicine men, or healers to visit a sick person at an IHS facility. This is an arena where strides have been taken to bridge the world of biomedicine with traditional healing.

Overview of Social Context and Sociolinguistics

Having set up the broad background of the development of Western biomedical culture and how it affects Indian Health Service settings and belief systems, it is now necessary to present an analytical framework to set up the structure of this inquiry. Overarching social theory of habitus must be looked at in order to locate the role of linguistic activity. It is important to establish theoretical distinctions between habitus, worldview, and culture. Once social construction is in place, sociolinguist theory, the nature of cross-cultural miscommunications, and the particular role of Indian English as it relates to health care communications can be addressed.

Habitus: Social Settings and Interactions

Because people experience the social world using language, they deliberately and continually "formulate reality through reference, description, and a variety of other speech functions" (Hanks, 2000, p. 1). The unconscious capability of language to objectify an "outer" world is offset by an equivalent capacity to embody the cognitive, affective, and corporeal orientations of individuals. Thus, to speak is inexorably to situate oneself in the world, to take a stance, to connect with others in a process of production and exchange, and to occupy a social space. Therefore, it is critical to be alert to where individuals are positioned and how their social context shapes their actions in encounters at health facilities on Montana's Indian reservations.

In its generative structure and use, language is one of the central vehicles of habitus. This is true not only because it provides the process of objectifying and infusing aspects of social reality apart from itself, although this is a significant function. Even more important is the fact that language embodies and makes routine social orientations that constitute habitus. More than just a tool for describing the world, language, no less than perception and bodily motion, is a means of access. Objects talked about are thereby made available to individuals under certain conditions, and the act of speaking itself constitutes a "presence" in a particular space in which practice takes place. How do these and other processes of meaning construction that occur through language contribute to social practice more broadly, and how do social facts mold linguistic practices?

The premise that linguistic practice takes place within a "market," according to an "economy" of exchange, that language is a form of symbolic capital (Bourdieu, 1982b, p. 140), and that utterances are formed according to the combined constraints of habitus and the social field[46] contribute to a comprehension of meaning production that cannot substitute for a semantic description. Language is produced, learned, distributed, and exchanged according to social factors. The social factors, markets, and economies on reservations fall at the low end of the social scale and, without these benefits, have a negative impact on Indian interactions.

Linguistic habitus in particular is initially acquired when children learn to speak; most importantly in a family situated in a discrete position in the social space. It proceeds to rule both linguistic

---

[46] Calhoun, LiPuma, et al. 1983; Bourdieu, 1985, 1988; and Calhoun, LiPuma, et al., 1993.

practices and the anticipation of the value that linguistic expressions will receive in other fields, such as the school, the work force, in legal situations, or in medical settings. The sense of value of a culture's own linguistic expression is an essential dimension of their judgment of position in the social space—it governs the expressions produced and the very relation adopted to different markets or social contexts, reflecting membership in particular communities.

Speech forms represent particular social groups and portray the group's interests and orientations through style and content. This orientation is central to the recognition of class variations and the resulting structural differences of their inherent power, limiting or expanding them. Indian communities typically represent class, social group, and style variations of conditions of poverty, disempowerment, and marginal class dispositions. According to Bourdieus's theoretical construct of habitus, class variation implies distinctions in the form of expressions that depend on the formality of the occasion that is based on the social distance between the speaker and the receiver and on the capacity of the speaker to respond to this tension with a suitable expression (Galfarsoro, 1998). The more "formal" the occasion, the more control is exercised on speakers outside the dominant language or the dominant mode of language use in any particular social context that is inherently linked to institutionally established relations of power, such as biomedicine.

However, there can exist contradictory forces that push participants to develop a degree of familiarity with more than one position in both social space and linguistic habitus, as is experienced with Indians who move freely, to various degrees, among Standard English, Indian English, and their traditional language.

Thus, society is composed of individuals, each with a mind and various arrays of private experiences and motivations. Differences between cultures serve to cause discord in language and understanding, and thus eventually result in failures in both communication and health care. It is only because Indians and non-Indians alike subconsciously agree to a shared common code that signals consensus of ground rules, often due to effects of Indian assimilation into the dominant culture and language and, due to consensus, that communication takes place at all.

Because words are separated from natural reality, convention is the necessary socializing factor. Therefore, if made-up words were to be spoken, no one would comprehend them, and conversation would cease to be true language and would ultimately degenerate into nonsense. "Semantics is the system of the ideal speaker-hearer, the system of conventions that everyone must learn in order to derive propositional content, successfully convey implicatures, and perform felicitous speech acts" (Hanks, 2000, p. 147).

To say that it is mutual conventions that make communication possible is to assume that speakers and hearers share an identical system. It has been established that clinicians and most Indian patients do not. There are two discrete concepts here: first, the idea that commonality among participants is necessary for successful communication; and second, that what is shared is the linguistic system. Regardless of its appeal for describing particular kinds of communication among small groups of similar people, the perception of a unified language community on which it rests is too simplistic. It disregards the rights and abilities to know differentiated and specialized patterns of usage that may prevent or confuse their exchanges with others but nevertheless do not prohibit them. Even a structure such as Bernstein's (1972) intricate and limited codes, Brown and Gilman's (1972 [1960]) early work on pronoun usage, or Gumperz's (1972b; 1982a) research on speech communities as set in social context, all point in the direction of differentiation.

If Bourdieu is correct in suggesting a struggle and competition over symbolic capital,[47] and language as a form of that capital, then an awareness of aspects of discord, breakdown, and conflict should follow, not merely as negative cases that support convention, but as central to the production of meaning. The reference to production of meaning (Hanks, 1993, p. 148) is significant in this context, since conventionality leads to the further assumption that the semantic

---

[47] Bourdieu's notion of capital, which is neither Marxian nor formal economics, involves the capacity to control one's own future and that of others. As such, it is a form of power. This notion of capital also serves to reconcile individual and society. On one level, society is structured by the differential distribution of capital, while on another level, individuals strive to maximize their capital. This does not mean that there is a purposeful preference they seek to maximize. Rather, unaware of some true possibilities, unable to take full advantage or conceive of other possibilities due to their class habitus, individuals nonetheless seek to maximize benefits, given their relational position within a field. The capital they are able to accumulate defines their social potentials; moreover, it also serves to reproduce class distinctions (1977, 1982a, 1982b, 1983).

system is predetermined in the sense that it exists prior to any occasion of its initiation.

This, then, serves to hide the critical idea that speakers innovate frequently, yet use language in highly effective ways, since language is produced, learned, distributed, and exchanged in accord with social and linguistic habitus. Social life, Bourdieu argues, must be understood in terms that "do justice both to objective material, social, and cultural structures and to the constituting practices and experiences of individuals and groups" (Calhoun, LiPuma, et al., 1993; Greco, Sweeney, Broomhall & Beasley, 2001). At reservation health facilities, the social and linguistic habitus reflect both Western culture and biomedicine as the macroculture that likely overpowers the microculture of Indian social structures.

Durkheim (2005 [1938], p. 86) established that ways of thinking, acting, and feeling exist outside the individual consciousness. These types of conduct or thought are not only external to the individual but are, moreover, endowed with coercive and constraining power that exists in the social realm. The political structure of a society is merely the way in which its component segments have become accustomed to live with one another. If their relations are traditionally intimate, the segments tend to fuse with one another, or in the contrary case, to retain their identity, as is the struggle of Indian cultures. The type of imposed habitation is merely the way in which contemporaries and ancestors have been accustomed to construct their houses.

Sherzer points out that discourse also has to be considered as the concrete expression of the language-culture relationship, because it is discourse that "creates, recreates, focuses, modifies, and transmits both culture and language and their interaction" (1987, in Sarangi, 1994, p. 414). Culture is commonly defined as the learned and shared patterns of knowledge, experience, beliefs, values, attitudes, meaning, roles, and concepts of the universe that a group uses to generate meaning among its members, encompassing non-verbal language and material goods (University of Manitoba, n. d.).[48]

---

[48] This is an excellent source of information on culture, cultural determinism, cultural relativism, cultural ethnocentrism, manifestations of culture, layers of culture, measuring cultural differences, reconciliation of cultural differences, and recent publications on culture.

Worldview

Worldview (Geertz, 1973) is a system of interrelated assumptions and beliefs about the nature of reality, the organization of the universe, the purpose of human life, religion and other philosophical matters that are concerned with the concept of being (Jain & Kussmanin, 1997, pp. 89-97). Habitus is the *active* engagement and *generative* enactment of worldview. Worldview concerns a culture's orientations toward ontological matters, exploring how and why aspects of culture derived. Worldview is a powerful, although tenuous, determinant of intercultural interactions. Deeply buried in every person's mind, most people take their worldview for granted. In the process of seeking health care, Indian worldviews can collide with practices of dominant mainstream culture and biomedicine.

Because worldview operates in such a latent fashion, communicators are apt to believe that people from other cultures see the world as they do. Ethnocentrism is the inability to believe that other cultures offer viable alternatives for organizing reality (Klopf, 1991, p. 98). When another culture with different values and assumptions, is encountered, it is not acceptable to think that it is as valid, since to do so undermines people's identity and leaves them without a frame of reference. The mainstream American culture is thus largely an ethnocentric one. The ethnocentric view causes misunderstanding of microcultures within national borders and in international politics and policies as well.

Culture

Cultures are particular. They have determined customs, behaviors, and populations, beginning with the largest concept of culture down to a small or isolated unique gathering of like-minded people. Each Indian tribe in Montana has a unique history, ceremonial and ritual practices, oral traditions, origin stories, language, and beliefs about health and the causes for its disruption. It is important to locate an Indian tribe in the context of the culture at large.

Soon, when demographers' computers once again spew out the latest data about the ethnic complexity of the United States, the predominantly Anglo-Saxon visage of the nation's founders will have all but vanished. Instead, the emerging population statistics will show an accumulation of races, ethnic groups, and immigrant populations. Intermingled in the population, the statisticians will find a grouping of 21 percent who will claim mixed ancestry (Klopf, 1991, p. 3). Already, the union of races and ethnic groups has brought change in the American way of life and will continue to do so in the years ahead. These fluctuations are not just physiognomical or skin-color differences. They concern the very nature of the country, immigration, its intermingling of people, cultures (food, clothing, religion, etiquette), languages, and behavior that constitute the national pool.

Racial and ethnic diversity is a global reality. With the increase of intercultural[49] contact of a physical sort, the mental distance that can divide cultural groups can become exacerbated. Real or imagined controversies can multiply, necessitating a concentrated effort to understand people whose backgrounds and beliefs widely differ. Variations in cultural behavior can result in our perceptions of customs of other people as peculiar. Most citizens in a pluralistic country share to some degree the macroculture, dominant, or mainstream culture (Klopf, 1991, p. 39).

The microcultures within each macroculture have distinct cultural patterns not common to the macroculture. The dominant culture, or macroculture, in the United States is Anglo-Saxon, a designation loosely used to denote any of the people of, or the descendants of, the peoples of the British Isles and includes the Danes, Normans, and Germanic tribes, among others. The United States macroculture, therefore, stems from political and social institutions in-

---

[49] By stressing "intercultural" aspects, the implication is that groups or individuals in society stand apart and interact from group to group, whereas by stressing the multicultural composition of society, this aims at the integration of the various groups (Dirven & Putz, 1993). It is no coincidence that the use of "intercultural" is more strongly represented in confrontation-oriented countries such as the United States. Alternative terms are used such as "interethnic" (Gumperz, 1978), "interracial" (Erickson, 1979; Rich, 1974), "transcultural" (Romney & D'Andrade, 1966), "transracial" (Smith, 1973), and "cross-cultural" (Hall, 1966; Hall & Whyte, 1960). These terms all denote slightly different aspects of the wider field composing the contact or comparison between two different cultural communities, which may or may not happen to be different ethnic or racial groups.

fluenced by Western European traditions. Marcrocultures and microcultures combine to shape the individual's worldview and influence interactions with others.

The notion of "culture" is very much contested in many modern societies, since both dominant and dominated groups often resort to "the culture card" in managing their power-maintaining and power-acquiring purposes. It is not always a one-way street where Indian individuals are more impoverished and the recipients of social prejudice, and the clinicians are stakeholders of the social elite, though most often that is the case. The comments from this non-Indian clinician describes how assumptions work both ways:

> *The people here think that they're not being understood because the people here live in poverty and that we [clinicians] all come from rich, wealthy backgrounds and there's talk like that. I know in one of the urban Indian cities they made people take a little class and read a book on how people in poverty look at things differently and things like that, and I know that many of the non-Indian employees were kind of taken aback because they came from worse poverty than most people knew. In my case, too. Poverty that was far worse than it is here. I think the assumption here in a place like this is that none of us understand poverty because we all come from the dominant culture and we all have this and that, and if they can't get something, some places it's because of racism, whereas it's actually a matter of money and they don't realize what it's like. I mean with my background, too. My feeling is not so much about culture shock about seeing all these people with poverty, but it's being kind of jealous in a way because, with my upbringing, of all the things they do have. Their cultural mindset is more one of poverty and oppression rather than the Indian traditions of the past, and they assume that this is true poverty and they have no idea of how it's not, and they don't realize that a lot of the people that work here, like me, come from below this and they think that we're all coming from above this to come here. But nobody here really talks to anybody about that because I think it would be incomprehensible.* —Ken (non-Indian clinician)

In examining encounters between the dominant and dominated groups in a multicultural society, it is necessary to subscribe to a dynamic view of culture. "Rather than attribute communicative breakdown to cultural differences in an unproblematic way, the analysis of intercultural encounters should aim at coming to grips with the workings of 'culture in individuals' discourse practices" (Sarangi, 1994, p. 416). Otherwise, different cultural attributes of participants can only serve to reify cultural differences in an essentialist way.

If allowing comprehension of another culture does not occur between doctors and patients who occupy different positions in the culture of biomedicine, (medical) linguistic competency, or historical and social conventions, then they tend to hold even more strongly to their familiar stance, while denying the alternative position. It is critical that clinicians and Indians begin to learn to comprehend one another's cultural linguistic and social practices in order to overcome the enormous gaps between them.

The link between meaning and social life is complex. The cycle of interactions can be explained by understanding that the "differential use of language yields different interpretive strategies, partly via the now familiar indexical mechanisms, partly by further processes . . . whereby specific linguistic features invoke the very context on interpretation to be employed" (Gumperz & Levinson, 1996, p. 360). Complex social systems breed communicational subsystems with barriers and different evaluations of expressive performances. Speakers of the same language are fractionalized by interpretive subsystems linked with distinct social networks in complex societies and, conversely, can have social networks that transcend cultural and grammatical systems to create shared interpretive systems beneath linguistic diversity.

It is important that these layers of unconscious meanings, cultural context, social networks, and linguistic behaviors be understood in light of habitus to realize just how complex intercultural encounters are as one attempts to analyze communications between Indians and clinicians in health care. Without an underlying notion or comprehension of habitus, communicative failures remain unattached to social theory and its implications, as well as isolated from health beliefs and practices.

In Indian health care settings, Indian patients and non-Indian clinicians come from completely different realms of social, health, and linguistic habitus. These differences are most often invisible and unrecognizable, but the gaps in understanding and communicating are sometimes experienced as devastating losses of life and well-being to a people who are already at risk of poverty, unemployment, and illness.

Sociolinguistics

The patient-clinician relationship is also governed by the effective use of language. Along with clinical reasoning, observations, and nonverbal cues, skillful use of language endows the history of biomedicine with its clinical power and establishes the medical interview as the clinician's most powerful tool.[50] Language is also the means by which a physician accesses a patient's beliefs about health and illness (Kleinman, Eisenberg, et al., 1978), creating an opportunity to address and reconcile different belief systems.

One of the measures of medical communications is how much and what kind of information gets transmitted. The need for information rather than treatment may actually be what brings patients to health professionals (Snow, 1993, p. 129). Some go only for a diagnosis, some go for ailments that are new, and others go to make sure a condition is under control or to confirm that their own treatment regimen is working. Furthermore, it is through language that physicians and patients strive to achieve an empathic connection that may be therapeutic in itself (Suchman & Matthews, 1988).

Without effective use of language, the doctor-patient relationship is seriously impaired (Woloshin, Bickwell & Schwartz, 1995, p. 727). To communicate meaningfully with patients, clinicians must have some understanding of the culture they serve. Improved clinician-patient communication means better care in any language. Therefore, the distillation and application of sociolinguistics is critical for improving not only the communicative strategies but also health care and the quality of life at reservation health facilities.

---

[50] Hampton, Harrison & Mitchell, 1975; Lipkin, 1994; and Lipkin, Quill & Napodano, 1984.

These fields of study are necessary tools for promoting communications in health facilities on Montana reservations.

• Communicative Competence

Whenever conversation takes place, a framework is constructed upon which participants must respond and deal with what is on the mind of the other. When analyzing encounters between the dominant and dominated groups in a multicultural society, it is useful to subscribe to a dynamic view of culture. "Rather than attribute communicative breakdown to cultural differences in an unproblematic way, the analysis of intercultural encounters should aim at coming to grips with the working of culture in individuals' discourse strategy" (Sarangi, 1994, p, 416).

The subject of intercultural communicative encounters is becoming increasingly relevant in light of recent interest in multicultural and immigrant societies. The relationship between language and culture is explored in the analyses of intercultural communication and addresses the question of how speakers "in intercultural settings [both institutional and informal contests] re/construct cultural differences and cultural identities" (Di Luzio, Günthner, et al., 2001, p. vii). Hymes (1962, p. 102) feels it is important to investigate the pattern of speaking in its own right so that systematic descriptions can give rise to a comparative study of the cross-cultural variations in a major mode of human behavior (or a "comparative speaking" entwined with comparative religion, comparative law, and the like) and give it its place in theory. This would contribute to other studies of the formation of personality in the early years and the study of speech as a factor in cognitive and expressive behavior that leads to concern with the ethnographic patterning of the uses of speech in a community. This is a major area that begs to be addressed.

Communicative competence is what individuals need to manipulate in order to communicate effectively in culturally significant settings, and refers to the ability to perform (Gumperz & Hymes, 1972a, p. v). There is an attempt to distinguish between what speakers know (inherent capacities) and how they behave as members of communities as incumbents of social roles and to explain their use of language to achieve self-identification with which to conduct their activities.

When individuals speak the same language but belong to different cultural groups within one society, they do not share the same ideologies and rhetorical or stylistic conventions concerning the realization of particular communicative genres. Some behavior across cultures is plagued by conduct that is not only influenced by the culture in which one develops (by enculturation or habitus), but also possibly by other cultures impinging from outside (through acculturation). To these early formulations has been added a psychological component—the changes individuals undergo during the acculturation of their group; this has been referred to as psychological acculturation.[51]

Some key elements of acculturation are: (1) there needs to be contact or interaction between cultures that is continuous and first-hand; (2) the result is some change in the cultural or psychological phenomena among the people in contact; and (3) there is activity during and after contact that is dynamic as the result of a stable process that may also continue to change in an ongoing process (Berry, Trimble & Olmedo, 1986, pp. 291-293).

Gumperz (1982a; 1982b; 1972a) brought the concept of misunderstanding into the discussion of what he called "interethnic communication," but problems arise in intercultural communication that cannot be fully described, either phenomenologically or theoretically as "failures," even when pragmatically specified concepts of failure are being used (Rehbein, 2001, p. 173). In intercultural communications there are many areas of ambivalence and fuzziness. It is necessary to identify the countless patterns and natural sequences of behavior that occur when people come into one another's presence and to see these events as subject matter in their own rights. Due to such differences, there may be communicative differences that result in incorrect diagnoses or medications for health problems that are not properly defined or treated.

---

[51] As a concrete example, think of students in a single high school, some of whom take Advanced Placement (AP) courses for college credit and study for the SAT or ACT exams that require a high level of vocabulary and mathematic skills compared to those who do neither and do not plan to continue their education.

• Indian English

Growing numbers of Indians in the United States speak varieties of Standard English as their first language. While this may be so, the context of conversation has significant Indian cultural and social aspects which lead to distinctively Indian interpretations and meanings (following Eades, 1994c). Although the chosen language code is frequently English, there are important pragmatic continuities in the ways language is used. By focusing on aspects of language use, some of the continuities that are significant both to the issue of Indian identity and also in developing effective intercultural communication will be illustrated.

Discussions of sociolinguistics show that language is much more than a reflection or expression of society and culture; it is a dynamic and creative instrument of social action. Such a framework is a powerful tool in understanding why people interact with each other in the way they do, including their intentions, and can also explain aspects of intercultural miscommunication in interactions where Indian and non-Indian speakers are using varieties of English.

In this country, there are many varieties of Indian English (Leap, 1993, p. 1). In some cases, linguistic details are quite similar to those found in the English of their non-Indian neighbors, coworkers, and classmates. More commonly, Indian English shows extensive influence from the speaker's ancestral (or "native") language tradition(s) or from other language sources and differs accordingly from non-Indian notions of "standard" grammar and "appropriate" speech.

Variations in Indian English include differences in vowel and consonant pronunciation; differences in pitch, stress, junctures, and tone; and differences in word and sentence structures.[52] Since most of these tonal varieties cannot be assessed in written accounts, it then becomes necessary to elaborate on examples that can be shown in transcription, as the written version of oral language. There are several differences between Indian English and SE, but they do not apply to all Indian speakers. First, there is a difference in frequency of plural and possessive suffix marking the possessive references and subject-verb agreement such as:

---

[52] See references for Cook & Sharp (1966), Fletcher (1983), Miller (1977), Kwachka (1988), Penfield (1980), and Alford (1974).

There's three way of breathing . . .
One of that medicines is . . .
Sometimes it's almost 20 patients, man and women together . . .
They is all here . . .
It's about this doctors here . . .
The doctor, they . . .

Indian speakers also almost uniformly add plurals to mass nouns such as "furnitures" or "homeworks."

Articles and pronouns are also used quite differently than in Standard English, may not be used at all, or may not match the subject:

She asked doctor for medicines . . .
This germs, they get into your cut . . .
This new doctors . . .
One of this days . . .

Differences in verb tense markings are noted in Indian English as mismatched according to Standard English constructs:

This nurse she come up to me and she said . . .
So him and his sons come over and asked them what they
    are doin'. . .
Well, I guess she go to the pharmacist and she asked for
    medicine . . .

There is also often a lack of subject-verb concord, which can be noticed in much of the interview material provided in this investigation:

There are some gossips that goes on over there.
The women has no choice to make.
The doctor don't take the case.
All the talks that goes on like that occur in the waiting room.
When the man get together, they have a lot of talking.

Sometimes prepositional choices don't match Standard English practices or are left out altogether:

He got fired of his job.
They were at fishing.
You wanna go bathroom?
She go hospital.

Another common difference is the construction of right-to-left syntactic constructions of word orders in sentences:

They drink pops is what I see them do.
What he is doing there is he is waiting.
From our parents is where we learn to give respect.

These differences in sentence structure are normally understood in the general meaning of a conversation. However, there are often social values given to "incorrect" SE, where speakers are thought of as unintelligent, underclass, "other," and when the actual content or context is devalued by speakers of SE.

It will be clear that sounds and sound sequences, word structures, sentence forms, reference contrasts, and approaches of metaphor and imagery are not the same for all Indian English codes. In fact, many American Indians claim to be able to identify speakers' tribal background simply by listening to their English (Leap, 1993, p. 4). The community-specific ties between Indian English and ancestral language grammar help account for these conditions. Many examples of the above notations of Indian-English usage will be found in the following transcribed narratives.

Such conditions have changed greatly since the colonial time of "pidgin" English (ibid.), which was a form of simplified language made up from elements of English and Indian languages used as communicative tools between speakers whose native languages were different. Indian self-determination and tribal empowerment, along with the popularity of Indian bilingual education, other programs aimed at ancestral language renewal, and the entrance of American Indians into education, linguistics, and anthropology have shifted the goals of Indian language research and broadened the interests of scholars—Indian and non-Indian—who are now active in this field.

While English has a lengthy history in Indian country and individual members of Indian speech communities may have been speaking English for some time, community-wide English fluency is a relatively recent phenomenon for many tribes. Indian English is the first language learned by two-thirds of today's American Indian youth, and for more than two-thirds of them, Indian English is the only Indian-related English language that they know (Leap, 1993, pp. 281-282).

Other functions of these codes—such as the role in child socialization, the recasting of contemporary ideas in traditional terms, representations of tribal loyalty and Indian identity, and ties to the urban language make Indian English a valuable resource for other segments of the tribal speech community. Indian English fluency becomes problematic for speakers in classrooms, the workplace, courtrooms, health facilities, and other settings where SE or the urban or mainstream language (non-Indian English codes) sets the "standards" against which fluency and proficiency are to be judged.

Equally important is the need to study situations where Indian English discourse takes on particularly powerful significance. These include settings such as classrooms, hospitals and medical facilities, police interactions and the legal system, and businesses such as the Bureau of Indian Affairs (BIA), post offices, and supermarkets. The connections between Indian English fluency and economic development should not be understated. Indian English fluency surely affects speaker prospects for employment, job security, and job mobility in the world of Standard English speakers. There are noticeable linguistic similarities in the narratives presented in this investigation, representing Indians from all of the tribes in Montana. It is also a mistake to be distracted by assumptions of similarity. Indian English sentences may resemble constructions found in nonstandard English, but the ancestral language base (habitus) underlying the Indian English code makes it unlikely that the surface-level similarities derive from similar causes (Leap, 1993, p. 284). Therefore, the habitus of Indian English is quite different than mainstream Standard English, though they may both appear to "sound" or "mean" the same thing. Indian English accounts for a great deal of miscommunication between Indians and non-Indians and for difficulties in discussing charged health issues from differing perspectives of competency and identity.

3
RESERVATIONS, DEMOGRAPHICS, HISTORY, KINSHIP

There is a considerable cross-cultural research tradition in medical anthropology, particularly on the links between communication, medicalization, the social construction of illness, and the disparagement of folk beliefs.[53] There is also extensive research of general sociolinguistics across cultures and as it applies to workplaces and institutions.[54] Over the past 35 years, although there has been a great deal of work on medical communication,[55] almost nothing has been directed toward cross-cultural assumptions about sociolinguistic differences between Indians and non-Indians.

Because misunderstood linguistic assumptions based on differing influences of habitus and the cultural practices of Western biomedicine affect the interview process between Indian patients and their clinicians, decisions about health treatments and outcomes can be negatively influenced. Specific linguistic miscommunications surfaced in the narrative interviews with Indians and non-Indians, patients and clinicians, that closely examine intercultural differences in both language use and health beliefs that originate from conflicting models of habitus, worldview, and culture.

A general review of the cultural material setting of Montana reservations is assessed in reference to the demographics and socioeconomic conditions that have shaped the historical events of policy and disease. Kinship relations will be considered since they impact social, economic, and family systems that interact in all linguistic encounters.

Once the underlying characteristics of the setting have been laid out, the data will shift to more closely examine particular cross-cultural sociolinguistic phenomena. Data from ethnographically structured interviews and field notes reveal distinctions in both verbal and nonverbal linguistic enactments of linguistic habitus. The verbal

---

[53] Farmer, 1982; Kyasanur, and 1987; and Scheper-Hughes, 1988.
[54] Dirven & Putz, 1993; and Scollon, 1985.
[55] Roter, 1989; Simpson, Buckman, M., Maguire, Lipkin & Novak, 1991; and Stewart, 1991.

qualities brought to light include the use of narratives and questions as means of seeking information, the tendency to agree with a questioner regardless of veracity, politeness and respect, silence and silencing, interruptions, confidentiality, and gossip that reflect issues of power and trust.

Nonverbal data highlight communications involving eye contact, touch, modesty, proximity, and constructions of time. Nonverbal behaviors are as critical to linguistic behaviors as verbal interactions, and often less recognized or researched. The concept of time is especially important for this study as it overlaps all other areas of inquiry with direct implications on linguistic behaviors.

Reservations

Montana is home to seven reservations that house nine tribes in addition to the Little Shell, who are a large but landless tribe.

1. Fort Belknap — Assiniboine and Gros Ventre
2. Fort Peck—Assiniboine and Sioux
3. Blackfeet Reservation (one of the ten largest tribes in the nation)—Blackfeet
4. Rocky Boy Reservation—Chippewa and Cree
5. Crow Reservation—Crow
6. Northern Cheyenne Reservation—Northern Cheyenne
7. Flathead Reservation—Salish and Kootenai
8. The Little Shell, though landless, includes the Métis (Chippewa and French) and is one of the largest tribes in Montana.

These reservations include approximately 8,292,289 acres of land within their boundaries, or nine percent of Montana's land base (Bryan, 1996, p. 20). Reservations in Montana have enclaves of government housing, with other homes in the countryside that are sometimes isolated from neighbors, and settlements in border towns just outside the reservation. It is not unusual to find multi-generational extended families living in single dwellings ranging from private homes, federally funded housing, to trailer homes. Family bonds can be a source of strength and knowledge as it is in this family:

*We have many families that are just maybe 20 people liv-
ing in a home with several generations. Like the woman, the
daughter, the granddaughter, the great granddaughter, four
generations living together.* —Quail (Indian patient/clini-
cian)

Some families live clustered in more isolated rural areas of the
reservation, which makes it difficult for them to be able to get transportation to health facilities when needed or for clinicians to reach
them by telephone, because telephone lines may not reach their
homes. Others live in neighboring border towns or have moved to
cities for education or work. It also means that clinicians must have
access to information for living arrangements in order to make contact about health related matters.

*The other thing is there is the housing community, the
housing development about maybe 20 homes. A lot of people
are going to be living out in the country. If you're looking
for someone, she may be way out and you wouldn't know
where she lives. [You'd have to find] somebody and ask
where they're at, but then you would know pretty much
where certain families live. Usually certain families kind of
live in a neighborhood.* —Quail (Indian patient/clinician)

In addition to crowded conditions, poor transportation and lack
of telephone service, there are also tremendous obstacles to Indian
families who need health care and for clinicians who try to contact
them. Because there are neither public transportation systems nor
paved roads to isolated sections of the reservations, getting to and
from health appointments or walk-in care is a problem for many,
especially if the clinic is located some distance from the home. It is
not unusual to have a two-hour drive to get to a health facility, making it unlikely that ill persons will make the effort to get treatment
before it is absolutely necessary, as these narratives illustrate:

*Not everybody is going to have a phone, not everybody
is going to have a working car. And the crowding, several
families may live in one house. You won't be able to contact*

them by telephone, they probably won't keep their appointments, because they have no way to get there. —Quail (Indian patient/clinician)

[Y]ou're talking about real difficulties that people have. I think they have to do with the conditions people live in. For example, if you have unreliable transportation, you have multiple responsibilities, you have a long distance to travel, or no telephone. All of the [these] and there are all kinds of things. You know fairness is something that you balance against mercy, which is that the person can't get there because they've got to drop off so and so and the daycare won't take them until right on the hour, etc. We deal with that every day because of the conditions in which we live, which means because people, it's very hard to be punctual when everything is mitigating against it. [We] just don't have good control of our own lives because of the limitations we operate under and those are economic limitations. —Teresa (non-Indian)

Try to go out on the rez and have to live a week, like live far away without a toilet working, trying to scrounge a ride to get in [to the clinic] for a sore throat, have to go through a long, you know like you don't have insulin so you can sit in the waiting room for the whole day, and you can then wait another three hours for pharmacy to fill it, and then you have to go and try to find someone to take you home. Some patients travel great distances to come in. I [think], do you realize this person came 70 miles to see you? It's a very hard choice in life, getting on insulin is something [to] struggle with for years and now you're giving them all this hassle about it. Then, to live with substance abuse or to live with a lot of people, you can tell they don't understand. There's like one patient who was going to leave because she didn't have anybody to watch her other children. And they [clinicians] couldn't understand why the rest of the family, she has a huge family, why can't somebody in that huge family watch those children so this poor mom can stay with her sick baby in the hospital. Families don't function that way. Some of them do, but a bunch of them don't, so you know I think there's a lot of. . . . Like that over-crowded home, so many different scenarios going on, all extremely stressful. And all the little children that belong to all different parents, one person who is very sick trying to hold it all together with very little money. But then there are other families that know their priorities are just different [from mainstream values]. They're not going to have a nice yard because that isn't a priority. Driving to every pow wow is something very important. —Sapphire (non-Indian clinician)[56]

These stories highlight how difficult living conditions on reservations interfere with making and keeping health care appointments that many non-Indian clinicians are unable to appreciate, causing friction and contributing to lapses in communication based on values that are neither understood nor shared.

Poor diet (convenience stores, fast foods, and commodities) due to inadequate sources of fresh meats or produce on reservations is a significant contributing factor to the high prevalence of diabetes and other dietary health conditions that plague reservation populations. Compounding poor food options is the traditional value of generously feeding family members and friends, which, while strengthening communicative bonds, serves to exacerbate Indian health problems. Clinicians cannot hold mainstream expectations for Indian patients, as these individuals illustrate:

They have a dietician[57] that is trying to get healthier foods . . . instead of your starchy, you know. If you're poor,

---

[56] It is compelling to note that some of the non-Indian clinicians who live and work at IHS facilities for long periods of time, participate in community events, and spend time with families, really do get to know what is going on in the culture around them and are welcomed as part of the culture. That is how they work out so well and are trusted by Indian patients.

[57] The availability of reservation grocery stores is minimal, often with a mini-market serving a large area. This means that there is a scarcity of fresh produce and meats, which leaves residents to rely on fast foods, sweets, soda pop, and "junk" snacks, exacerbating health problems linked to poor nutrition and diabetes. Since it is a cultural norm to be generous and to serve visitors food, people stretch their budgets to provide for family, friends, and strangers who stop by their homes.

starch goes a long way, carbs, let's face it. Fruits and veg-etables aren't part of commodities. They're trying to change commodities too. They say, okay let's have some perishables too. But they're not really commodities. But if you live on commodities, you got a lot of flour and sugar and fat and cheese and whatever. —Emilie (Indian patient)

[Y]ou can't make certain expectations that aren't cul-turally appropriate. For instance, you have to eat when you go to places, so even though they have diabetes, they're not going to turn down the food, even though their diabetes may be totally out of. . . . It's an insult for them to say no to someone. When there are graduations, they may have four, five, or six parties in one day. And they will not just have cake and ice cream, they'll have the full meal with the cake and ice cream. There are certain things, and if somebody, say, is on a limited budget, someone comes to their home, they cannot refuse, say, "Oh, we're eating now, come back later." No, they must invite them to come in, so for this rea-son they make larger amounts of food, not knowing who may show up. Then, if they don't have company, they finish it up. —Paula (non-Indian clinician)

Partially due to high unemployment and historical causes and practices, Indians who are unemployed are more likely to consume high levels of alcohol, drugs, and cigarettes. Alcoholism is respon-sible for many of the accidents, deaths, and illnesses on the reserva-tion. Alcoholism contributes to poor communication ability and poor reliability for keeping medical and other appointments. Along with complications from smoking and second-hand smoke, these factors interfere with maintaining good health and safety for patients and those around them. A lack of understanding on the part of clini-cians contributes to stereotyping and making assumptions about In-dian health that may not be true. The results of unemployment on health issues is explained by this patient:

As far as what I feel in having communication problems with IHS doctors is more like they're on a reservation set-

ting and there's up to 80% unemployment on some reserva-
tions, and when there's poverty, I think, there's other prob-
lems that are created by that. You know, like alcoholism and
such, maybe domestic things and, um, so I think that [clini-
cians] have a hard time relating to that because. . . . As far
as interfering with health care, I think the [clinicians] frus-
tration leads to sometimes not treating their patients appro-
priately. —Brigette (Indian patient)

Direct continuity can be seen from pre-colonial times, when extended families were provided for by the labor of tribal members
with an obligation to share certain portions with specific kin. What
is more significant than the extent to which resources such as
money, housing, and cars are valued is the expectation that they will
be shared. This is certainly an area in which both Indian and non-
Indians perceive a great cultural difference that, like diet and alcohol
consumption, is not understood in the context of biomedicine. Non-
Indian clinicians may not grasp Indian values, attitudes, intentions,
and actions without understanding the fundamental pivot of kinship
relationships, particularly it impacts the seeking or neglect of medical attention.

Demographic and Socioeconomic Conditions

Major contextual barriers of health communications between
clinicians and patients include prejudices that clinicians hold about
poor and minority patients, differences in medical knowledge and
health beliefs between clinician and patient, and variations in communicative framing and cognitive reasoning. Clinicians often perceive poor and minority patients as lazy and noncompliant, which
"can viciously undermine constructive communication between
doctor and poor patient" (Ventres & Gordon, 1990, p. 306). This
perception is well understood by patients and they have strong reactions against such discrimination. It is not a far leap to see that these
perceptions influence diagnosis and treatment of illnesses:

I see that some non-Natives think that Natives are stupid
and some people that work at the hospital think that . . .

they're stereotyping, they see a lot of alcoholism but they don't see the rest of it, they don't see, they only see the bad because they work in a hospital, they don't see the good out there because they don't go out there and intermingle and see what it's like and see the culture and see the religion, they only see the alcoholics, therefore all Indians are alcoholics, drunks, and no good. —Jackie (Indian patient/clinician)

Acting through the agents of poor housing and nutrition, debt, forced taxation, education, economic opportunity, media influence, and greater environmental risks, lower socioeconomic position and minority status are associated with poorer health and shortened survival (Lantz, House, et al., 1998; Sorlie, Backlund, et al., 1995). As sovereign nations, when Indians live in poverty due to forced government controls in business, education, agricultural economics, and land ownership policies, they sometimes have no choice but to accept government welfare and food commodities. These conditions not only contribute to the erosion of sovereignty but to socio-economic and minority disparities in the process and delivery of health care (Andrulis, 1998) and communicative skills.

These factors are not a reflection of choice but of circumstance. Efforts to carry forward traditional cultural values in the face of the pressures of assimilation are a challenge to survival. The resulting tension between opposing worldviews adds one more layer to the difficulties in communicating across cultural boundaries and divided concepts about health care, as this patient so eloquently reports:

I think that [Indian] people have been trying to [become educated and linguistically competent] since day number one—since the very first interaction with the Whites. I think they understood that we can't give up what we have, but we have to learn what these people do, because that's the only way we're gonna survive. And I think that's the touchstone that people have tried to get to—that they've tried to retain their culture and get an education. And I think in the [Indian] culture, the people who've tried to do that have really been respected and held to high esteem, held up as role models, and there's been a lot of 'em. I think that there's an appreciation and an acknowledgment in the [Indian] culture that education is something that you have to have. But I think that there have been so many problems— social problems, poverty, substance abuse, alcoholism, I mean there're all these other things get into the mix.

And so I think it's been harder and harder to keep that touchstone. Because now you're losing the culture. Used to be that kids grew up with the culture, and then their achievement was to gain knowledge of the White world through education, and then you'd have both worlds. Now kids aren't growing up with that same sense of cultural knowledge or the same type of cultural immersion. Because things change. And I guess there's many reasons for that. One reason is the fact that more [Indian] people are marrying outside of the tribe. They're marrying people who don't speak [the traditional language]; they're marrying people who don't practice the traditions. And so you've got mixed culture families who aren't necessarily as traditional as the generation before that. —Alan (Indian patient)

Since socioeconomic positions, as measured by education or income, are clearly related to standard measures of health care quality (Fiscella, Franks, Gold & Clancy, 2000, p. 2579), it is therefore necessary to incorporate views of language, society, and power that are capable of dealing with questions of access, dominance, disparity, and difference. Language plays a crucial role in the construction of such differences. "[A]ccess, power, disparity, desire, difference, and resistance" (Pennycock, 2001, p. 6) require an historical understanding of how social relations developed. Additionally, when individuals enter the presence of others, they commonly will be interested in information about others, including "socioeconomic status, conception of self, attitude toward the speaker, competence, trustworthiness, etc." (Goffman, 1973, p. 1). They will also bring preconceptions that affect the communicative process in ways that linger long after the initial encounter as this patient points out:

If two people are in a room, a Indian and a White, they're going to perceive each other by what they already *think as a stereotype, you know what I mean? So, if a Indian girl is sitting with a White girl and the Indian girl's being very quiet, you know, the White girl's gonna probably perceive that this girl is to be either brow-beaten or very shy or very introverted or . . . even rude! But what they might not think about is this person's just sitting here! That's all they're doing. They're just sitting here. You know, I mean, that doesn't mean anything about me or how they perceive me. But in our culture, the way someone treats you is automatically, that you're talking to me or whatever. But I should try to clarify that what I'm trying to say here is there is a lot of opportunity for doctors to misunderstand their patients and to assume things and that's how relationships get created and stay that way.* —Alan (Indian patient)*

A central and continuing source of frustration exists because the gifts and talents of minorities are not only unrecognized but also frequently denigrated by members of the dominant society. It is the corrosive daily frustrations and the inability to communicate or establish meaningful relationships that contribute to "soul-shrinking" (Hall, 1976, pp. 6-7) when communicating between institutional cultures. It follows that there are contextual problems that are embedded within the communications between clinicians and Indian patients in the institution of health care. For much of the public, Indians have historically been understood as stereotypes of savage, noble, wise, spiritual, alcoholic, or other varieties of new age or misinformed biases that are referenced by mainstream views and media. Part of the breakdown in health communications rests on such unfounded perceptions, while assimilative forces have incessantly chipped away at Indian cultures for so many decades, as is further elaborated:

First of all, first and foremost, the [Indian] culture is not what it used to be. If it were, then you could expose it to all kinds of things and I think that it would probably stay strong and stuff like that, but because it's not what it used to be, then all these little things can affect it. And so, when you get kids who aren't speaking [the traditional language], and you get kids who are growing up on the reservation, all of

the information they receive from the mass media has noth-
ing to do with being an Indian. Well, then, the kids begin to
think about their future and about the world out there, and
they realize that being an Indian really doesn't have any-
thing to do with that. Well, that's when they start to say, well
maybe I should either act like this, or this is what everybody
else is doing. When I grow up, I'm gonna have to be like
this, or this is what the cool people have, or this is what the
rich people have, or what the powerful people have. This is
what the smart people have. This is what the good people
have, and it's not what we have! And I don't see what we
have anywhere! It's not reflected on television and we don't
see it in the books. I don't see it on the movies or turn on the
radio and hear it. I don't go anywhere [in the city] and see
it. And so, what you have is kids living on a cultural island.
—Alan (Indian patient)

To avoid living on such a cultural island, there must be cultural
and communicative exposure and training for clinicians who work
on reservations. Unless medical and health training programs are located in areas that are densely populated by Indians, practitioners at
best take one course on multiculturalism or doctor-patient relationships, and only a small portion, if any, of such courses are devoted
to the study of Indians. Therefore, most medical practitioners who
come to work in IHS facilities and Indian communities have had
almost no training about Indian culture, health beliefs, or doctor-
patient communications.

Indians who are sick become especially vulnerable and anxious
when visiting clinicians who hold social power. This leads to a propensity toward breakdowns in communications, especially when patients understand that doctors have accrued status built on years of
training and expertise, along with the cultural capital that accompa-
nies it, and the ability to make critical health decisions about the
patient. This dichotomy of position enlarges already existing gulfs,
as brought forth:

Anybody feels anxious when you go to a doctor because
nobody wants to be sick and all this and that. All the discom-

*fort factors and then the rotten kind of training and commu-
nication that contemporary doctors are given no matter
where they are, the idea that they are superior, the idea that
they've suffered more than anybody else has suffered, and
therefore they deserve more. Just the fact that they belong to
a different economic class creates a barrier, so then you're
getting down to what might make more of a barrier.*
—Teresa (non-Indian)

From the perspective of a clinician who works at a reservation
facility, clinicians are often as frustrated as patients. Some clinicians
have an awareness of cultural barriers and know that there is not a
pan-Indian behavior that explains all Indian behaviors. Cross-cultural training was absent from the training of the clinician below,
but he learned what he could from on-the-job experience. He reports
that further cultural information is unnecessary for him and that
there is no time to learn more. This attitude seems to reflect a pre-
disposition to practice the tenets of biomedicine without a deeper
understanding of the background of the local patients being treated
and how they respond to biomedical practices:

*I understand, there are things I'm still learning about
their culture, but I find it's mostly because it's not a universal
thing. Some of the elders adhere to certain of their practices,
others adhere to other parts of it, a lot of the young ones don't
participate in any of it. Traditions. And their understanding
and their approach to medicine, their approach to life, their
approach to traditions and wars, superstitions or non-super-
stitions, what's good life, what's bad life, that type of thing. I
haven't got it all by any stretch of the imagination. I don't
have a real thorough history of their background, their native
history. There's just books and books based on it, and I've got
enough books to read, I don't need that.* —Evan (non-Indian
clinician)

Most clinicians have had minimal cross-cultural training or instructions regarding doctor-patient communications. However, the
irony is that, though training is unlikely to provide a very broad

spectrum of divergent cultures, it also does not often reflect the immediate microcultures in direct proximity to the health facility in which the clinicians being trained actually practice. This point is not lost in this clinician's narrative:

> *[Cultural training] wasn't a lot. It was pretty superficial saying there was a difference in cultures and acknowledging that it existed. There was a lot of insular communities of Black people, White people, Italian, Polish, whatever. Some of them didn't mingle too well, but nothing was really brought out. Most of the time it was just kind of lip service to different cultural things. One place where I was working, some Mormons came in and the nurses were starting to have a real conflict about how much [clothing] to take off and everything like that—their temple garments and things like that, and after I told the nurse what all was involved there, and after the patient was gone, she said, "You know, we get classes on being aware of other people's culture and talk about Arabs or who knows, people we never see, but people we do see, nobody's ever told us about that stuff, and if I'd known this, you know, I wouldn't have had a conflict."*
> — Ken (non-Indian clinician)

The technical vocabulary of biomedicine practitioners, lack of direct time with patients, and specialized approaches to problem solving further add to the communicative asymmetry between clinicians and patients in which both parties become communicatively incompetent in achieving mutual understanding:

> *[Sometimes a doctor will ask] a question like, "When was the last time you had your period?" We call it "moon." There's a difference in the language. If I said to somebody, well when was the last time you had your period, that's scary to people, but if you said when was the last time you were on your moon, then the answer would come right out. Because it's familiar and that's how you say it. "Period" is a term not used here, so terms have a lot to do with the questions you ask.* —Jackie (Indian patient/clinician)

Just like when you're trying to explain your symptoms and like they just kind of seem to accept them fast, like they already know what you're talking about and stuff, and maybe they take and get the whole description out, and then when they explain to you what's going on they can sometimes use big words. Like words you don't really know what they're talking about. —Carla (Indian patient)

Clinicians and patients have different senses of what is expected and accomplished in medical interviews. Eisenberg (1977) notes that doctors communicate about disease observed through biomedical investigation and that patients communicate about illness and the perception of what is wrong and its meaning. The way clinicians think and conceptualize clinical decision-making and their view of patients' lack of formal knowledge about disease is often confusing and frustrating. The social class of patients is found to significantly associate with provider behavior. Poor and minority patients receive less information about their conditions, less positive or reinforcing talk, and less talk or communication overall than do patients of higher socioeconomic classes (Hall, Roter & Katz, 1988). The poor who are ill may also adopt a passive stance that does not reflect their concern (Bain, 1976; Waitzkin, 1985, 1989). Indian patients' experiences are also worsened by the rapid and constant rotation of physicians who are strangers to the patients:

Not knowing something [caused fear]. A lot of times, the doctors, when they're finished, don't tell the patients everything. They don't tell them what's wrong with them or how to solve the problem, and with a lot of that, plus we have doctors that come in and stay with us two weeks and leave, and when you have a lot of that, you're kind of leery about talking to a doctor, and especially when you go home, and you don't know anything, and you think, okay maybe if I take some medicine or maybe if he would explain it to me or say that I would get better. —Jackie (Indian patient/clinician)

Historical Events That Influence Indian Health

History is intricately tied to cultural identity, and it shapes and affects current perceptions and behaviors. As recent as the 1960s-70s, women were forced to undergo unauthorized sterilization at Indian Health Services and Job Corp agencies as a form of racial population control (DeFine, 1997; England, n.d.; Lawrence, 2002). Spinal tap experiments were performed that sometimes ended in death, and perhaps over half of Indian children were ripped from their homes to be placed in boarding schools whose aim was to enforcedly strip them of their language, culture, and religious practices to compel them fit in with White culture. Indians' trust in institutions plunged lower than ever, and skepticism remains today that biomedical practices can be a form of experimentation on a marginal population rather than therapeutic treatment:

> *One thing that always is a problem is doctors wanting to do spinal taps on special children, and that's very upsetting to the parents and the family . . . so they usually will say no. It's just colic, and they seem to be really upset if you do anything with the spine. I never did really ask anybody exactly what's upsetting about that. One time I heard that they did it to somebody and it paralyzed them. So I know being paralyzed is a fear. It's really upsetting. You see that pediatricians come here from somewhere else and they're really baffled about the spinal tap problem and they really are convincing somebody they really needed to have it done.*
> —Sapphire (non-Indian clinician)

Historical incidents that shape and affects patients' perceptions and behaviors are important to consider when working with Indian individuals and their families. The racial genocide that Indians endured has contributed to their identity as a population and has created a mistrust of White professionals (Trimble & Medicine, 1993pp. 312-313). Large-scale factors of genocide, forced assimilation, the removal of ancestral lands, and the outlawing of traditional practices have largely stripped Indian ties to past cultural and health practices. There is a collective sense of loss and grief. "Researchers have increasingly tied the erosion of Native American cultural and environmental resources to declines in tribal health."[58]

Increasing Indian exposure to English as the standard language suggests practical problems associated with decay of Indian languages and assimilation (Labov, 1972, p. 183). Hymes elaborates that "domains of language use have been described as 'the occasions on which one language (variant, dialect, style, etc.) is habitually employed rather than (or in addition to) another'" (Fishman, 1966, p. 428). Parallel structures of overpowering biomedical and linguistic practices dominate Indian health beliefs and linguistic traditions. Such losses serve to lessen the importance of their historical roots and cause them to use a new language and a different approach to healing the ill by treating illness as a physiological abnormality separate from natural and spiritual realms.

Kinship

The spiritual integrity of the Indian extended family system is an explicit tribal concern (Red Horse, Shattuck & Hoffman, 1980, p. 2) and represents the fiber of a social fabric that binds families and communities. Clan membership, for example traces lineage, organizes patterns of relationships, establishes social obligations, and serves as a social control within tribal society. The pervasiveness and importance of kinship and taboos for most Indians is in constant evidence and serves as the base for individual and social identity (Schwab, 1988, p. 80). Kinship bonds are often confusing to non-Indians who do not know how to interpret familial connections through the use of linguistic terminology for relations.[59] Respect

---

[58] Brian Bienkowski, "Sacred Waters" in Environmental Health News, September 20, 2016, http://www.envronmentalhealthnews.org/chs/news/2016/tribal-series/menonimee-series/river-fight-boosts-a-tribes-long-threatened-culture.

[59] Kinship data derived from ethnographic contexts apply to communicative data as well as to kinship data (Conklin, 1964, pp. 25-26). Kin terms are almost in continual use as they reflect actual relationships and as indicators of affiliation and affection where no traceable kin relationship exists. For example, the term "uncle" reflects an extension of kinship to include persons whom non-Indians in similar relationships might not consider kin. Certainly Westerners can and do

among kin plays a central role in Indian social, political, spiritual, and linguistic arenas Almost every individual interviewed presented information on the role of kinship and how it related to their interactions in the medical setting.

> *Family ties are very strong! First impressions are very important. First of all, in any culture is respect. You have to have respect for the people and their family. Not only the person but then learning the culture. Men to men is more comfortable. It's more men associate with men, women associate with the women.* —Vine (Indian patient)

Kinship data derived from ethnographic contexts apply to communicative data and kinship data (Conklin, 1964, pp. 25-26).

> *I think it will just vary with how the doctor treats a person and it's probably like doctors are adopted[60] into families, which I think is a smart thing because then you can access that doctor easier. Because he's your brother or your uncle or something. But still they form a bond with that doctor because usually doctors like it that they got adopted in and so, if you call, they're not going to put you on hold forever, they'll call you back because you're their brother. And usually that doctor has done something helpful or something that they admire.* —Sapphire (non-Indian clinician)

Brown and Shaughnessy (1980) use a concept of the "dual perspective" to explain how Indian families cope with the values, attitudes and behavior of the larger societal system. The dual perspective refers to a nurturing system (the family and/or tribal community support network) and to the sustaining system (that is the dominant high culture as expressed by the schools, the BIA, IHS, economic resources, political power, etc.). Congruence between the two, they state, would be supportive for the family and incongruence between

---

make such fictive extensions, but less frequently than do Indians, where such extensions serve to anchor both individual identity and the Indian community's identity.

[60] It is not uncommon for Indian families to adopt non-Indians whom they feel close to and want to include them in family and ritual activities.

the two would result in messages of inferiority, conflict, and racism. The sustaining dominant system does not serve to support families who struggle either with dysfunction or success, as this patient reports:

> *Just like grown-ups, you treat our children with respect. Because they're our relatives. We all have winos in our family and we did not like what they done to our cousins or uncles or whatever. . . . Made them awful. I'll just talk about two or three or maybe more, was the fact that they had all this training and we're just poor little old Indians and we don't know anything. No matter who has gone to college and who is a doctor themselves or whatever, they, oh no. . .*
> —Karen (Indian patient).

It becomes critical for Indian families to develop two ways of relating and coping through bicultural adjustments, whereby Indian families maintain strong traditional values and also acquire the skills and means to succeed in the larger society as well. Ideally, the Indian family provides the power that produces bicultural identities rooted in tribal and kinship systems. Given this power, Indians can move with ease into the sphere of technology without loss of harmony and self-esteem within their family. The process of higher education necessarily includes inculcation of mainstream skills and thought processes. Fortunate enough to be strongly grounded in her kinship relations and cultural traditions, this patient explains why she can navigate both worlds without losing her cultural grounding:

> *So one of the things that I've known in my years of experience is that our [Indian] culture is a very healthy culture. And that's why it was so easy for me to use both [Indian and non-Indian] cultures, but then never lose my true culture.* —Quail (Indian patient/clinician)

The manner in which Indian culture is created and reflected through ways of communicating, language becomes an integral part of social action that is distinctly Indian. Since English (or Indian English) is the language primarily spoken, aspects of the way it is used reflect and help to maintain and create a culture that is Indian and shows continuities with traditional Indian cultures. Health care professionals must be aware of the importance of relationships and networks that may affect an individual or family. In a very real sense, for the majority of Indians, kinship remains the foundation of identity.

4
VERBAL MISCOMMUNICATIONS

Medical encounters involving doctors from one cultural group and patients from another are cross-cultural in nature. Fuller and Toon (1988, p. 1) note, "The doctor must know about the culture and background of the patient, and must be able to speak across the cultural and linguistic divide." This requires a purposeful attempt to step enough beyond one's natural habitus to be open and to experience another. It is a task rarely accomplished.

Effective communicative skills are key factors in achieving satisfactory clinician-patient interactions that affect both satisfaction and compliance in the system of health care, with implications for cross-cultural practice. Fuller and Toon (1988, pp. 1-3) outline basic elements that contribute to satisfactory communications with and understanding members of other cultures in order to provide optimal care. Cross-cultural medicine entails more than clinical facts; it must also include cross-cultural knowledge of social systems, thought and communicative patterns, and beliefs about health and healing.

The clinician must be able to uncover and define and then deal with an Indian patient's concerns and expectations with knowledge of the patient's health-belief system and the patient's family background and socio-economic and living situations. The clinician must also be able to engage in a respectful, warm, and friendly manner that reveals a sincere concern about the patient and includes a matching of verbal and non-verbal cues, a positive feeling toward patients (and their family and cultural group), a matching of their expectations of each other, and coincident areas of concern. Whether the clinician gives information in a way the patient can understand is another factor contributing to satisfactory communication.

Additional factors of satisfactory communication include the patient's previous experience with the clinician (or with clinicians in general) and the view of clinicians held by the patient's cultural group (for instance, there is some evidence that close-knit, self-sufficient communities view clinicians with greater suspicion than less close-knit communities). Because Indians have a history of negative encounters with federal and state governmental politics and health-related policies of bodily invasion, it is safe to venture that mistrust of non-Indian doctors exists, especially for patients who are older or more traditional. All of these elements are markers for potential miscommunications.

Personal Narratives and Questions

"In successfully identifying and understanding what someone else is doing we always move towards placing a particular episode in the context of a set of narrative histories, histories both of the individuals concerned and of the settings in which they act and suffer." —Alastair MacIntyre[61]

It is not unusual to think of an ordinary daily narrative as a teller constructing a story[62] for the listener. Accordingly, the typical way Indians present information is through narratives that give the speaker control of the story and lays out information in a logical manner. A primary means of giving Indians control over their own health care would be to allow for (and to *elicit*) the use of narratives, allowing speakers to present a full story of their illness or concern in their own words (Clark & Mishler, 1992). The effective practice of medicine requires the clinician to have narrative competence, that is, the ability to acknowledge, absorb, interpret, and act on the stories and plights of others. The teller is supposed to make the story coherent and interesting and to impart information to the listener.

In settings where biomedicine has not repressed forms of Indigenous health care, storytelling plays an integral role in the management of health and illness (Smyth, Gould & Solobin, 2000), especially where there are large areas of minority or immigrant populations. Importantly, storytelling provides a vehicle for clinicians and their patients to mutually engage through a common cultural context and to communicate about matters of personal significance that cross boundaries between illness, well-being, and another culture's rich traditions of story and narrative in healing. In order to carry this

---

[61] Kleinman, 1998, page 272.

[62] Story, like narrative discourse, is a representation but, unlike discourse, it is not encoded in material signs. Story is a cognitive construct with a mental image that concerns certain types of entities and the relations between these entities. Narrative may be a composite of story and discourse, but it is its ability to evoke stories in the mind that distinguishes narrative discourse (Ryan, n.d.).

out, the tellers perform a variety of simultaneous tasks (Barry, 1993, p. 203): They assess the listener's knowledge of the topic. They signal foregrounded or mainline story events from background information. They trace the identity of referents to prevent ambiguity and misinformation; and they signal relationships among events, either temporal, causal, or otherwise, by choosing appropriate connectives. The listener's job is assumed to be more passive: to take in the information, to provide appropriate signals that the narrator has made the right choices, and to ask for repair when needed.

If Indian patients experience the health facility as impersonal, they express their need to find a comfortable way of easing into their health concerns with clinicians who are often strangers, younger than themselves, or not particularly informed about Indian cultural practices, beliefs, specific health issues, or the historic and current ability to talk in stories (or narratives). Clinicians who have been on reservations for some time have tried to adapt to what they often feel is irrelevant patient information that takes up time but also affords patients the opportunity to open up, as this clinician recounts:

> *I've got a number of the elders when they come in and all they really want to do is just talk, and I'll just kind of catch that real quickly, there's nothing wrong with it, but they just all of a sudden want to talk to you and tell you about something in their life, the history of their people. I'll just sit back, have a good time. [I wasn't trained], but I mean that I picked up on that or that I had several patients come through do that, and I thought, oh they're trying to tell me something. No, I've done that from the very beginning. Some of them start telling me stories, they'd ask me questions, what did I know and what do I do because I was new. And then they'd start telling me stories, interesting things. One guy was saying he wanted to take me out to the backcountry, and he wasn't so sure it was a good idea or a bad idea . . . take me out in the backcountry, and he was telling me you could hear all the natural sounds and you could hear the coyotes howling. They'd be howling all the time, the wolf and coyote. And then I had another one who was a singer, traditional drummer and singing, and he sang to me a healing song. He kind of sensed that I was pretty*

anxious with work and that type of thing. So I just sat back and listened and relaxed. It was very nice. I enjoyed that approach. I still try to get to it in the first visit. It may take longer, instead of it being a 20-minute appointment it may end up being 40 minutes before they get to it. Surprisingly, that's their time to feel you out. They'll take the time to sit down and talk with you and get a sense of where you're coming from, and then they'll either come back to you or they won't. —Evan (non-Indian clinician)

In addition to narratives, indirect or broad questions help to put patients at ease and provide a beginning point to launch a narrative, though it is not always apparent at first what the relevant information actually is. Stories tend to spiral around the main point, while at the same time shed light on the heart of the matter. Sometimes clinicians recognize the Indian paradigm as different than the Western paradigm—more psychologically- or sociologically-based than biomedicine as this clinician clarifies:

Sometimes a couple questions open somebody up, and they'll start talking about something else. Otherwise, we can just sit here and look at each other. Or maybe not even at each other. They may look at the floor. I don't think for the most part they like to feel interrogated. I think the questions have got to be limited to a few. If I don't know the patient, I might just say what brings you in today? So they can talk about it, and they might say I don't have a clue. For instance, everybody goes to the doctor, the nurse comes in and gives you this form and they may ask you 50 questions. That is sometimes, a lot of people feel very intimidated, you don't want to go that route. So I think a lot of them do want to tell the story, however, sometimes I've taken the motivational interviewing type, and the thing about it is, most professionals have been trained to get a lot of impact in a short amount of time, and that is very turned around. That is more like a psychologist, sociology type approach, and all of a sudden, it's what the person, your

client, your patient, wants to talk about that day you're fo-
cusing on. And it may just be a very narrow little bit of what
you really wanted to give. —Paula (non-Indian clinician)

Questions are often necessary for clinicians to confirm the information they need or for clarification of a narrative and background
about people, especially in concerns about the time, place, and setting of an illness or episode. Indirectness is typical of Indian conversations, where the questioner presents a proposition for confirmation or correction. Being indirect is counterintuitive for clinicians
who are pressed to obtain quick answers within a very short visit
with their patients. Time also constrains patients who wish to speak
in the narrative style that they are comfortable using. Narrative reports are more expressive for Indian patients, who often feel that
clinicians are not listening, but focused on their own agendas. Sometimes a combination of narrative and questioning works best, as this
Indian patient suggests:

I think you could start out that way [with narratives],
but then I would like whatever they tell you, I'd like ask 'em
more questions about it to make sure you're getting like the
whole picture and like seeing everything that's wrong.
'Cause I know, like, man, there's like so many stories back
home where people that go to the doctor, and they [doctors]
just kind of like brush 'em off and then they end up having
like something serious. —Carla (Indian patient)

In fact, if questions are used to chop a narrative into small pieces,
with the assumption that the reassembling of the pieces forms them
into a "whole" story, a critical misunderstanding may ensue. The
clinician below describes her experience of both the efficacy and the
drawbacks of patients' narratives for eliciting information:

The cultural part is the story, is the important thing. That's
how they're relating their symptoms. Most of the time it seems
they don't come in with just real black and white, real
straightforward. I think [stories are] how they mark the time,
that's why it's important. One big problem is you're in a
hurry because you have another patient waiting, and another

patient, and that it is hard to get used to not listening and allowing them to tell a little story instead of just I came here because I have had a headache for three days. It's more like, three days ago when I was at the birthday party I started to notice . . . and then they tell a whole little story. And then when you think about it, it is kind of a good way because if you didn't remember it's three days ago, but you remember you felt funny at the birthday party. They won't be like that [sequential details], it will still be a story. It won't be broken down like that. And for some, especially the older people, it's going to be, they're going to feel like you're understanding them better if they tell the story, because that's how they understand it or that's how they're living it or something. Then you kind of forget why they're there, and you get all confused and it's hard to stay focused for me, because they threw in a story with all these other little things and you have to pull out what it is. There's plenty of younger people that will be pretty straightforward: I've had a headache for three days and I want something for it. But not completely. Sometimes if it's something more vague, maybe they tell more of what other circumstances were happening. —Sapphire (non-Indian clinician)

When patients were asked whether they prefer using a narrative rather than answering questions, many noted their preference to use their own words to describe the events leading up to an illness. Clinicians' questions can be experienced either as helpful to the patient in eliciting pertinent information or as being rude and inconsiderate, irritating, and off the point of the narrative, since questions are not necessarily the primary means of seeking information (following Eades, 1994a, 1994b, 1994c, 1995, 1996, 2000, 2002, 2003a, 2003b) in Indian communications, as the following patient reveals:

I just felt like they were asking me question after question. That's kinda how I felt. I didn't feel like I was given the [opportunity to tell my story] . . . just to ask us what happened, tell me what happened, how you feel, why you're here, what do you want? That's what I'd prefer, the story.
—Alan (Indian patient)

In situations where Indian patients are not familiar with the non-Indian clinician they are speaking with, the issue of mistrust enters into conversational style and the patient is assumed to be withholding. Interestingly, this patient suggests that clinicians should ask even more pointed questions for getting at important health details:

> *Natives will not freely give you information. If you want to know something you're going to have to ask that question in order to get the answer. This happens to us a lot. And later the patient will say, "Well, you didn't ask me that, that's why I didn't tell you." They're not going to volunteer, whereas in another society people just volunteer what's wrong; when it started, and they can give you whole paragraphs about it. But, for Natives, ask specific questions, you'll get the answer, and you may have to ask more questions in order to get exactly what's wrong with them. And you may have to broaden your scope on questions.* —Jackie (Indian patient/clinician)

Occasionally, narratives can also be a source of frustration for clinicians and patients if the narrative is not given directly by the patient or if another teller goes against the patient's wishes. This is more likely to happen when extended family members are involved in patient visits and hospitalizations. This patient's sister tried to speak for her sick mother who did *not* want her story told:

> *Just like my mother, she recently passed away from diabetes, and my one sister was living with her and taking care of her. She knew what my mother was going through and when my sister would tell the doctor [our mother's story], [my mother] would get mad at my sister for telling the doctor what's wrong with her, because she kind of give up on herself.* —Bannock (Indian patient)

The key element for all patients is the amount of comfort, trust, continuity of care, and rapport they feel with their clinicians as a corollary to opening up. Many have had to navigate both Indian and non-Indian worlds, and through those experiences and exposures to the media, they have become more and more expectant of questions and answers as the means for clinicians to quickly gather pertinent health information. The majority of Indian patients, in the end, still seem most comfortable with the narrative form during their health care visits.

> *We do both [stories and questions]. I prefer telling [stories]. I don't see the same provider every time, so it's different every time. Some do, some don't [allow stories]. But I prefer it when I can tell my story.* —Austine (Indian patient)

> *I prefer telling her why I was there rather than her asking me a bunch of questions why I was there.* —Diane (Indian patient)

> *I just felt like they were asking me question after question. That's kinda how I felt. I didn't feel like I was given the . . . time to just tell us what happened, tell me what happened, how you feel, why you're here, what do you want? That's what I'd prefer, the story.* —Alan (Indian patient)

> *It depends on if I feel comfortable with the person. Then I'd probably tell them my whole life story, but if I don't, I probably won't say anything.* —Dorothy (Indian patient)

With narrative competence (Charon, 2001; Loustaunau & Sobo, 1997), non-Indian clinicians gain the ability to acknowledge, absorb, interpret, and act on the stories and plights of others. There is no set amount of time it takes to tell about an event and the speaker determines the length of the narrative. Physicians can then reach and join their patients in illness, recognize their own personal journeys through medicine, acknowledge relationships with and duties toward other health care professionals, and inaugurate consequential discourse with the public about health care. This requires an ability to venture outside their own worldview of how biomedical consultations function in Indian health settings. It also disrupts any set time schedule. Since Indian patients, if given the opportunity, have an average of three concerns per office visit (Kaplan, Breenfield, et al., 1989; and Stewart, Brown, J., McCracken & McWhinney, 1986., the likelihood of overlooking critical issues and creating less efficient visits seems realistic. The clinician also assumes that because there are no questions asked that Indian patients are satisfied with their treatment; conversely, patients frequently describe satisfaction even though they understand little of what they heard (Pratt, Seligmann & Reader, 1957).

Often the medical approach ignores narrative and, along with it, the psychological factors of health and disease (Smyth, Gould, et al., 2000). Most people do not like to be interrupted, but for Indians who tell stories, it is especially disrespectful. The Indian approach to health narratives is closer to a bio-psycho-social approach to which psychiatry attempts to give lip service. The tension between psychiatry and the rest of biomedicine is reproduced.

Attention to the patient's story may provide a rich fund of information that will facilitate treatment in the dominant biomedical model. If there can be a shift beyond the boundaries of the Western perspective that typically frames storytelling as subjective and stories as anecdotes, narrated accounts can be shared in a clinical context between patients and practitioners as significant communicative and evaluative activities. Narratives can be seen as forms of knowledge transfer offering resources, topics for inquiry (Hammersley & Atkinson, 1995), and also strong concerns about life and death decisions. Almost all of the patients interviewed expressed frustration and anger that their stories weren't taken seriously and were treated as trivial. Just about everyone reported "horror stories" based on a primary lack of communication and consideration of narratives, such as this one:

> *I have a sister that's living on the rez and she was having, she had been very sick for over a month, and she was unable to eat anything or drink anything, and she was sustaining by going to the doctor and asking them to give her an IV of fluids, 'cause she was getting so dehydrated. And they ran a lot of tests on her, and they couldn't find out what was wrong with her. They sent her to [the city hospital]. They sent her to have a, they couldn't figure out what was wrong. Um. She doesn't drink alcohol and one of the doctors at IHS kept insisting that she must be drinking alcohol*

because of her symptom, and that was like very upsetting to her, because here she was, like, you know, on her death bed and they're insisting that she must be drinking alcohol to have these symptoms, and what actually had happened was her gall bladder shut down, so she was like getting liver problems. Her tubes shut down and bile was going back towards her liver, and she just felt totally helpless and stranded like [IHS] couldn't help her, they wouldn't do anything for her. They'd find nothing wrong through these tests. They actually ended up doing exploratory surgery [in the city] and fixing the problem, but then she would go home when they couldn't find anything when she was there, and she was literally like really hanging on by just a thread, and she would go into the emergency room. She just felt really helpless about it because they, um, were insisting she was doing something that she wasn't, like they didn't want to give her the help that she needed. They couldn't give her the help that she needed. I think [they were basing it on a stereotype], because I can't imagine going to a private doctor and having someone insist . . . [that you're drinking alcohol] and you can't even drink a glass of water! You know, why would you be drinking alcohol? And I know one time when she needed a medication and they had a new doctor, and the doctor was so frustrated because they didn't have any of the medications that she wanted to give her, and so she had to give her something really powerful that was kind of inappropriate because that's all they had. And I think that's kind of scary, you know, kind of giving what you have, not what you need. —Brigette (Indian patient)

Narratives in a clinical setting effectively communicate symbolic meanings by organizing health-related observations, actions, motives, evaluations, and outcomes into a healing context (Burke, 2000). This is critical in societies where Indians believe that illness and recovery are contingent upon adherence to culturally encoded rules that support personal and familial well-being. Stories that allow the ordering of temporal events and elaboration of relevant physical, emotional, social, and spiritual aspects augment and sustain meaning in the therapeutic situation (Slobin, 1998). Because so many patients feel that their concerns are not taken seriously, they assume it is because they are not being listened to due to lack of time, money, or interest in really listening to their medical problems. These failures in the communicative process can result in outcomes of life or death as this patient reports:

> *Like, there's another example of my husband's mom. She had like, really bad headaches, and she went to the doctor, and they just kept sending her home with like painkillers and saying it was just regular headaches and stuff like that. And that happened for like, I don't know how long, and then by the time, I mean it was like they just kept doing that, and then pretty soon she was having trouble with her vision and like falling and stuff, and it ended up that she had a brain tumor. But, you know what? They could have found that a long time ago, because she had all the symptoms and she told 'em, but they just kind of, they brush a lot of things off like that. Yeah, they always have to worry about financial and there's not enough money to go around to everybody, I don't think. And, like the thing with the brain tumor, that happened to more than . . . that's happened to probably three people that I know of back home, like them. Just like a friend of mine, she had a brain tumor, too, and they gave her, they kept sending her home for a headache for the longest time. So it's not like just a incident, it's like a thing that happens because they just don't have the money and they don't listen. —Carla (Indian patient)*

Despite the symbolic and literal importance of storytelling for Indian patients, however, there may be obstacles to the both generation and reception of relevant information in the medical environment. Findings from studies on patient-clinician interactions suggest that one in five patients ask no questions at all and that 13 percent of patient questions go unanswered (Hahn, 1995, p. 169). Clinicians in one study of biomedical consultations thought they spent an average of eight minutes providing information, when in actuality they spent an average of only 1.3 minutes doing so. For Indian patients, the potential for seeking information is even less.

A lack of information is problematic for patients, especially when their recall of doctor's explanations and instructions has been reported to be only 50 percent (Hahn, 1995, p. 168). Combinations of patients' reticence to ask questions (as impolitely challenging authority), answering questions that do not address their concerns, and time constraints serve to interfere with optimal information sharing, as this patient expresses:

I think they [doctors and nurses] have their own questions for you. Like there's times I left the doctor's office, and I didn't feel I got everything, and I couldn't get anything in that I had questions about. —Carla (Indian patient)

A patient's narrative is an integral component of the interaction that both reflects and reflexively informs and guides that interaction. To describe an Indian patient's narrative is complex, since it emerges in the context of requests, acknowledgements, expansions, and elaborations. Ideally, it represents co-production by the patient and physician to make coherent sense of a problem within a jointly constructed context of actions and results. By shifting the focus to a patient's active role in the discourse, it follows that there is a shift away from the physician's assumed role of power over the discourse and toward the patient's exercise of authority. Attending to the patient's story and incorporating appropriate questions clarifies how the task of biomedicine is framed within social relations in health care. Here is an example where the grandmother intervenes with the clinician on her grandson's behalf. Though again revealing patients' feelings of not being taken seriously, this grandmother's intervention clearly led to a better outcome:

Well, when my son was, he's 6 now, but when he was about 2 ½ years old, he was with his (he don't live with me), he was living with his mother. He had been riding in a pickup standing on the seat and when his stepfather turned a corner, he fell out the window onto the pavement, and it left a gash in his head about the size of a quarter, completely to the skull. They took him to the hospital [on the reservation], a non-Indian doctor seen him first and prescribed some Tylenol, kind of brushed up the wound a little bit and was trying to send him home. I wasn't there at the time. I was [in the city]. So my mother happened to be there and basically asked for another doctor to take a look at him. When the doctor came, it was an Indian doctor who ended up having him flown out to [the city] because there were gravel underneath the skin, up underneath the skin. And once he got to [the city hospital], he had to go through some plastic surgery and there was a lot more to it than just the Tylenol and the wound being cleaned up. There needed to be more done. —David (Indian patient)

Though narrative accounts of illness are preferred by most of the patients interviewed, questions are a reality of medical discourse that patients need to be aware of. Even in the asking of questions, there are cultural differences between Indians and non-Indians. Indians form questions by making a statement with a rising intonation such as, "That's where he fell?" This differs from the non-Indian word inversion, "Is that where he fell?"

It is often more useful to hint at a statement, followed by silence, so that the Indian patient may fill in information more easily, such as, "It seems as if . . ." However, because of the danger of agreeing to questions based on a sense of politeness, it is important that "this strategy does not amount to a series of thinly-disguised direct questions" (Eades, 1992, p. 39). Instead of asking, "Were you feeling feverish?" a better indirect strategy would be to ask, "You were feeling feverish, right?" Or, instead of directly asking, "Did he say how he fell?" substitute, "He said how he fell?"

A non-Indian clinician reflects on another difference in the phrasing and use of questions and distinguishes between "remembering" and "knowing" information:

There are a few things that they phrase a little bit differently here that you kind of have to watch. Well, instead of saying "you remember how this . . .?" when they're kind of just making a statement of fact. And, of course, there's no way that I could remember, because I wasn't even here, you know. Like, "you remember how the sun comes up every morning?" Whereas we'd say "you know how the sun comes up every morning?" —Ken (non-Indian clinician)

It has been noted (Philips, 1983, p. 126) that there is evidence of Indian patients' lack of comprehension or familiarity in the structure of discourse and questioning with physicians. When Indians answer non-Indian questions from the reference of their own worldview, frequent miscommunications significantly impact their health care. Among themselves, Indians often use indirect questions as a means of gathering information. Clinicians' indirect forms of questioning and waiting for a response is the best form of gathering information (Tafoya, 1989), but goes against the time-driven scheduling of bio-medicine's impersonal system that favors treating the location of illness rather than personal concerns.

In attempts to adapt to this system, Indians typically struggle with the questioning process and expect professionals to take a directive role in the information gathering, while also maintaining a general mistrust of White people and their questions (Brucker & Perry, 1998, p. 316). The following patient has had experience with doctors off the reservation and has become familiar with the use of questions. Some patients who worry about being put on the spot sometimes feel that direct questions would help to force more forthcoming answers:

> *I think for a lot of Indian people, men and women, men especially I think, that they aren't very comfortable talking about their health problems and they might leave the doctor to guess. I think like being really direct, it's kind of like putting the person on the spot. I don't know if [being indirect] would help, but I think it would be worth a try. I don't know how direct some of the doctors are, but it seems they've got to still be really, really leery of certain people. I think if you were really direct with me, I would probably be a little more honest about what was bothering me or whatever. I think being direct is really important. When asking questions, you know. I might be a little more comfortable just telling them what's wrong with me, you know. But I've been off the reservation and I've experienced other hospitals, and I know that ain't a big thing, but it's helped me to be a little more open. I would say [it's better to] be direct with those kind of people. The community where I grew up, people are really clannish*

there, and I think, yes, in that kind of situation, you'd have to be more direct [to get answers]. —Bannock (Indian patient)

While narratives give patients the chance to open up about themselves, questions that are open-ended can also be used as invitations for patients to use narratives. Such questions can be used to make the speaker feel comfortable and willing to share information, while noting that this is much easier within established relationships. The sometimes necessary use of short-term clinician rotations and "rent-a-docs" works against such strategies of health communications, as this Indian patient/clinician implies:

In my experience with us [Indians], [narrative] is an opportunity for them to finally talk about themselves. When I was a [professional], what you have to do is get their trust at first, but they do seem to enjoy those few minutes when they're able to talk about themselves. Because I know what you're saying, and I think sincerity and knowing that you're not just there for yourself, but that you're there for them. And you're not just some person with their own interests, but if you're sincere, they know it and then they trust you, and especially if they think this is going to help them get better or get some help, then they will open up. [My first question] usually it'll be more of a social thing. How are you doing? How was your trip? And if I know about your family or something and then maybe if you're an older person, I may talk about stuff that happened a while back. They like to talk about history or stuff in the past [to put them at ease]. [I don't think people like being asked a lot of questions], of course not. Preferable would be it'd be somebody they'd known a long time so that they wouldn't have to explain a whole lot of stuff. —Quail (Indian patient/clinician)

Though most people interviewed preferred to use their own words in a narrative to explain the reason for their visit and about their concerns, there is also evidence that patients are too intimidated to present their concerns and questions to clinicians because they don't want to waste doctors' valuable time or bother them with what they think may be considered unimportant questions.

Often, though, they are afraid not only to ask a question, but also to hear the answer, as this clinician describes when speaking of a vulnerable young mother with a sick baby who is suspicious of the doctor's information, thinks the doctor is judgmental, reacts defensively, and is unable to ask the questions on her mind:

Just like with the example today that I had. This young woman had a baby up in ICU in [the city] and the doctor kept being very pessimistic and it was very upsetting to her. He was probably trying to just give her information maybe, and it was not good information to hear, because she was being told that she had a [very ill] child or he had a little complication, and he was saying we may have to send your baby to [another state]. So she was hearing things that caused her great distress. She also said that he was just a very pessimistic doctor, and I told him let's wait a little bit, and she said he got really kind of upset with her. That seems to be hard, and I don't have it resolved either. If you give information that isn't good information or happy information, of course defenses kick in, but it seems like they take it personally. They think that you are giving them more of a bad outcome than it's really going to be.

I don't know if it's so much now, but they'll [Indian patients] say that you're [clinicians] wishing bad things upon them. I don't think she was really saying that he did wish bad things for her, but still it seemed more like he was very pessimistic, and he shouldn't have been. I haven't had patients who are non-Indian for such a long time that I'd know that any mother would probably balk. I think she took it more, she didn't ask questions, she took it more like he was, I think she probably was more silent and didn't verbalize her feelings about what he was saying. And maybe a non-Indian would at least say more, like wait, I'm really scared and things are moving too fast. Where she wouldn't say that, she would just keep it all inside and think that he's a very pessimistic doctor.

I think it's a mechanism more than anything. In general, [Indian patients] don't ask a lot of questions; they go by other cues rather than verbal. I think she'd even be kind of uncomfortable a little bit if you would say, "How do you feel about what I'm saying?" She might not be able to say, she might get really scared. You might have to say, " I bet you're feeling really scared about what I'm saying." That's a really touchy situation because it is very upsetting news.

They'd be pretty passive, so then you'd keep piling on more and more information and they're sitting there, who knows how they're processing it because they're not . . . and usually it's bad. Because like she said that she remembered everything the doctors told her and she was repeating it to me today, but she didn't ask the doctor the question that she asked me. You get all this information and think later about what to ask. —Sapphire (non-Indian clinician)

The rapid turnover of doctors contributes to Indian discomfort and mistrust because they feel new doctors have to start all over again taking a medical history and want to get through the appointment as quickly as possible and get on to the next one. Patients feel not only rushed, but treated impersonally. They may have opposing agendas, where the clinician needs to move rapidly to closure and the patient needs to build the background information for the visit. While trying to obtain information, clinicians may be detached and impersonal, causing the patient to feel insignificant, as expressed by this patient:

Like I said, I haven't been in to see the doctors very much, but the last time I remember going, the guy wasn't even looking to me when he talked. He was looking at his clipboard. Like, okay, how long has this been happening? You know, not even looking at me, just kind of looking at his information as he writes it down. —Alan (Indian patient)

Use of narratives versus questions can be worldviews apart in conception and practice. Health care interventions require both Indians and non-Indians alike to stretch beyond the comfort of their own linguistic habitus in order to meet the requirements of properly addressing and treating Indian health concerns. While Indians are more apt to be familiar with the custom of asking questions through their schooling and the media, non-Indian clinicians are rarely trained to understand the central role of Indian narratives in talking about their health.

My field note entries addressing the very process of using narratives versus questions were filled with frustrations with my own behaviors, even after months of learning about, practicing, and feeling prepared to switch back and forth between the two during my interviews. Here are some entries:

•By the time I turn on my recorder after explaining this project, how I will proceed, and asking for input, I feel we have already begun to develop a communicative rapport. I knowingly begin my interview with open-ended questions to draw out her stories. [She] begins by telling me "horror stories" about terrible things that happened to her sister and her friend, where she feels frustrated because the problems were caused by the clinicians who really didn't listen to the stories they told about how sick they were and what the problems were about. Her main frustrations are not being listened to and that the doctors thought her sister was "just another drunk Indian," when her sister doesn't even drink. There are portions of her story that stray off the topic. I have to remind myself that through her stories that may seem to wander, is where I am finding what I am looking for. Her stories are rich and valuable. They captivate my attention and make me angry on her behalf.

•When I begin to ask [her] specific questions, I receive shorter answers with less detailed or personal information. Questions are less successful in drawing out the full picture. Like many of the clinicians, I find myself at times impatient and wanting to get right to the point ("my" point in "my" world), and wanting to jump in with questions, as is my natural tendency.

•As much as I am aware of the importance of letting him tell his stories, it is difficult and sometimes frustrating to realize that I really am not prepared to gather information completely through narratives. More often than I am happy with, I interrupt and ask questions, while simultaneously almost kicking myself for doing so. I am sometimes unable to overcome my own training as a non-Indian "fast-talker" who wants to be direct and directive at the same time. I fall into the very traps I am writing about. I realize how parallel the dilemma is of me as a non-Indian researcher to that of many of the IHS clinicians.

•It is more of an art than I realized to be able to sit quietly and attend to the information by carefully listening and absorbing the whole of the process. I understand at these moments why clinicians and patients have a hard time adapting to each other's preferences in seeking and providing information. I realize how difficult it is for clinicians to break out of the mainstream medical habitus of talking and listening in a way that may not be actually communicating. I feel humbled and a bit like a child who can't sit still long enough to pay attention. This is a very different way of listening than I am used to and, and all the more, I admire the qualities I wish I had more naturally. I will make a point to listen more patiently in the following interviews and to see what I can learn about myself and the process of listening. I see that I am an interference to my own objectives, and how hard it will be for the most willing clinicians to change.

Gratuitous Concurrence

Since questions are an inherent aspect of biomedical consultations, most Indian patients deal with them the best way they can. This may mean skirting around the issue, hesitating to answer, pressure to rush, or feeling suspicious. Additionally, many Indians "will answer questions by White people in the way in which they think the questioner wants" (ALRC Report 31, 1986, p. 404). This communicative strategy of agreement, labeled "gratuitous concurrence" by Liberman (1981), is significantly underestimated in communicative practices between Indians and non-Indians.

Gratuitous concurrence is the tendency to freely agree to questions "regardless of either the speaker's understanding of the question or belief about the truth or falsity of the proposition being questioned" (Eades, 1994a; Liberman, 1981). The way in which appropriate levels of politeness are represented is a potential source of problems (Murira, Lützen, et al., 2003, p. 259), which might lead a patient to answer "yes" when the speaker really means "no" or "maybe."

Though courtesy and civility can do much to enhance a relationship and improve communication, even this form of expression may be culturally relative. For example, some Indian patients may not wish to bother nurses, even when in pain, for to do so would be disrespectful (Loustaunau & Sobo, 1997, p. 155). The tradition of being polite often causes Indian patients not to assert themselves, express their confusion, or ask for clarification with non-Indian clinicians, especially if they feel they have not had the chance to build up a personal rapport with the clinician. Agreement also allows clinicians to draw uncorroborated conclusions that can lead to incorrect treatments, as this patient provides:

I think it has to do with comfort level and knowledge of the person you're interacting with. I think for most [Indian] people, a lot of 'em, being agreeable is something you do with somebody when you don't know who they are, because you don't know how this person's gonna react. If you know someone your whole life and they say something to you and you don't want to agree with 'em, well then you feel comfortable doing that. So, in health care, if the doctor's asking questions, like, "So your stomach doesn't hurt today, right?" And you say "right," but if you have pain and you say "right," they're really missing the boat on communicating how you're really feeling. I think they are. You can't put words into people's mouths because, generally, they're gonna let you do it. And so I feel that you really need to let people say what's on their mind. —Alan (Indian patient)

The bond between agreement and compliance in reference to medical directives is often weak. Though patients want to appear agreeable, what they are being asked to do may be far beyond their capacity to change. Despite good intentions, there can be a lapse in following instructions they do not wish to hear. This non-Indian clinician expresses his concern and confusion about gratuitous concurrence:

What I find most problematic is trying to make sure the patient understands your instructions that you've told them. Some of them sit there kind of starry-eyed at you, or they sit there and nod their head, then they go out and do what they want to do anyway. So you don't know if you're getting across to them the instructions for them to change their life-style, or how to take the medications that you want them to, or understanding their disease process of their diabetes, or things along that line. Trying to ascertain that they really understand what you're saying, or are they just agreeing with what you said to get out the door. You can ask them to repeat back their understanding of what you said. I think is a good way for giving them certain instructions—for instance, how to take insulin. That can be complex. So I ask them if you get this, what are you going to do? If you get this kind of meds what are you going to do? Either [they're in a hurry] or I've lost them so completely in my instructions, that yeah, let's just get out of here, I'm confused enough, I'll try to remember what I've already heard or got out of the lesson. —Evan (non-Indian clinician)

Another clinician expresses her frustration in trying to determine whether an Indian patient is agreeing merely to be polite while also questioning if the patient understands the directives that need to be followed:

They would probably be nodding [in answer to questions]. [Agreeing] because the way you're saying it is it's real easy. They should figure out what you're saying, because it's just a real easy thing. Sometimes I'll say, let me hear, how are you going to take it? What are you going to be doing when you take this? Or are you going to be traveling? —Sapphire (non-Indian clinician)

Although there is often a sincere effort by clinicians to communicate with their patients, without knowing the linguistic and cultural nuances of response patterns, it is difficult to know whether there is actual agreement of assumptions and perceptions. Patient may readily agree to follow a diet or exercise plan at the moment, but go home and realize that it requires a real change in lifestyle to be made that they are not willing to make. It sounded simple in the clinic, but in practice it won't happen. Agreement in all cultures does not necessarily mean compliance, especially in Indian cultures, where agreement is so closely associated with politeness and respect for (or fear of) authority. Unless clinicians are aware of this propensity for their Indian patients to agree out of politeness, there will ensue misunderstandings and incorrect information that will significantly diminish appropriate treatment.

I noted some interesting occurrences in my field notes regarding gratuitous concurrence. Though my personal reactions were not as intense as in other areas of this inquiry, I fell into similar traps built from my own habitus:

> •After I ask him for his personal stories, I begin to ask him questions. I realize there are times when I wonder whether he is "agreeing" with me about what I'm asking, and I'm not really sure. At home, I don't have to wonder about this, because we all just argue our points. If he is telling me something that isn't especially useful to my research, I let it go. If my question is something I want to know more about, I begin to ask more questions to confirm whether what I think he is saying is what he means. A few times his information contradicts his initial answer, causing me enough confusion that I have to ask for further clarification. By doing so, I once again fall into the trap of asking a series of questions, which I know is not beneficial.

> On the other hand, I notice that when I ask him to clarify what he means, he seems to feel I am more interested in what he is really thinking, and he is glad to explain more. Though he seems a bit put off at first when I interrupt to ask a question, he also appreciates that I want to follow his thinking. I hate that I keep interrupting!

> •I purposely try not to provide any bias or direction for what I am asking to know about. Because of this, I think she doesn't feel I am judging her about anything she is saying so she can be more honest. There is also less reason to want to agree with me when I phrase my questions neutrally.

•She expresses suspicion about the motives and outcomes of my research after we discuss it at length. At the end of our interview, she decides she does not want to participate in the project and declines to sign the post-interview consent. She asks me if I will send her the transcript of her interview and says maybe she will change her mind. I tell her I will transcribe hers first and send it to her. I note that she clearly has no tendency to be agreeable out of politeness but exercises her own preference. I respectfully comply and withdraw her from my study after she declines to sign the post-interview release, but send her the transcription.

•Everyone is polite and respectful to me—a stranger and a non-Indian. I appreciate their acceptance, willingness, and confidence to participate in this inquiry and treat me kindly and with trust. A few people are a little aloof, but not what I'd consider cold or distant. Everyone wants to be helpful. Is being helpful part of gratuitous concurrence, I wonder?

•It is interesting to question whether I feel my own behaviors reflecting a tendency to agree with information or questions put forth to me. I have to distinguish whether *I* am being agreeable or confirming that I am listening, something I don't usually think about. It isn't always easy to tell, though there are certainly times I mentally disagree with what someone is telling me, or I feel the person is way off track in either their racial stereotypes or impressions of others' intentions. I feel personal biases from people, but I refrain from offering any judgmental feedback, as that is not my purpose or inclination. I find I favor some people more than others in my private thoughts. I am surprised to realize that I need to think about my own behaviors toward agreeing in order to be authentically polite. Though I had read a great deal about this tendency in Indigenous cultures, I hadn't thought it out in reference to my own behavior until I am here actually conducting these interviews.

Silence and Interruptions

Indian cultures have been identified as having a greater tendency towards silence than the dominant non-Indian norm (Basso, 1970; DeVito, 1998; Montoya, 2000; Tannen & Saville-Troike, 1985b). When most Indians do speak, they are not usually talking from the head, relating some theory, mentioning what they read in a book, or what someone else has told them. Rather, the more traditional they are, they may speak from the heart, from the traditions of their people, and from the knowledge of their land and origin stories. They speak of what they have seen and heard and touched, and of what has been passed on to them by the traditions of their people. These conceptions of speech and silence are not worldviews that IHS doctors have been trained to be aware of, and they serve as a major source of health care miscommunication.

Ethnographers and linguists have generally paid little attention to cultural interpretations of silence or to the types of social contexts in which silence regularly occurs (Basso, 1970; Hymes, 1962, 1974b). Although the form of silence as an audio channel is always the same, its function varies according to the social context in which it occurs. For a stranger entering an Indian society, knowledge of when not to speak can be as basic to the production of culturally acceptable behavior as what to say, for there can be no language or speech without silence, nor can there be silence without speech (Schmitz, 1994).[63]

Since speaking and silence live in a symbiosis and are dialectically dependent on one another in the role of silence, there is a large discrepancy in the use of and comfort with silence between Indians and non-Indians. Many misunderstandings are created in Indian health care facilities that impact the outcomes of health decisions precisely because Indian use of silence is virtually ignored.

A basic finding of sociolinguistics is that the usage of language is more structured than language itself, and the usage responds most sensitively to extra-linguistic influences (Ervin-Tripp, 1968; Gumperz, 1964; Hymes, 1962, 1964; Slobin, 1967). Because silence is nuanced and may be difficult to interpret, Saville-Troike offers

---

[63] *Eloquent Silence* (Schmitz, 1994) is an excellent resource for widespread information on linguistic aspects of silence.

the following negatively valued symbolic or attitudinal non-Indian assumptions about the nature of Indian silence as: nonparticipation, anger, sorrow, respect, disapproval, dislike, indifference, alienation, avoidance, mitigation, concealment, mystification, dissimulation, and image manipulation (1985, pp. 3-18). Other negative perceptions that occur outside the linguistic communicative habitus of silence include attributes of ignorance, confusion, evasion, insolence, or guilt.

The symbols of identity in Indian culture are powerful, but not necessarily recognized (and even less understood) by non-Indian IHS clinicians. Though there are positive values of silence, listening attention can also be conveyed negatively on the part of the hearer who receives a message (Philips, 1983, p. 9). The communicative competence involved in structuring listening attention is both productive (speaking) and receptive (hearing), (Philips, 1983, p. 46). Indian listeners typically provide less evidence of attention through responses to the speaker than do non-Indian interactors.

Because of this, Indian patients are often incorrectly viewed as shy, slow, or backward, and may be pressed to make rapid responses and immediate decisions before they are ready. Clinicians may become impatient with their slowness and deliberateness of discussion or take silence to mean agreement. This patient/clinician explains how silence can even be misdiagnosed as depression, mental illness, or as a lack of interest:

> Well, I've always heard "she's quiet." I was always described as quiet too. Especially now with a lot of the depression and the mental illness stuff, they might think you're a depressed person [or] it could be considered non-interest.
> —Quail (Indian patient/clinician)

Culturally aware doctors can try to assess the patient's nonverbal communication including amount of eye contact, posture, facial expressions, and signs of anxiety to provide support if the client acts anxious or fearful. Clinicians can encourage the client to initiate conversation by sitting quietly and encouraging the person to break the silence and communicate verbally. Clinicians in biomedicine work on very busy and pressured time schedules with short patient intervals that often hinder this option. Such tight scheduling does not afford Indian patients the time they need to think and reflect about either their narratives or their answers to questions. Because of this, they feel doctors think they are dumb or ignorant rather than respectful, and this is a frequent source of friction and misinterpretation for IHS doctors, as the following patient illustrates:

> *I think it took a while for the doctor to get used to me. Like, he'd ask me if I had any more questions, and I'd have to think a while for my questions. And it seemed like in that time I was thinking he was already done, like with asking my questions and stuff, when I was still getting ready to ask my question, and I don't know, I felt he kind of like brushed, before he kind of got used to me and working with me, he kind of brushed me out of the office fast before I was done saying what all I wanted to say. More like he [was in a hurry and] thought it was just a routine appointment and he just wanted to like get me out of there and, you know, get on to his next appointment and stuff.* —Carla (Indian patient)

The difference in role expectations is quite evident, especially in IHS settings. Indians resort more to listening behaviors, which are connected to showing respect and politeness. It also has historical roots in listening to long narrative stories during winter months. In the narrative below, it is evident that an Indian woman who is married to a non-Indian man speaks of Indian men as drawn-in and shy, compared to her husband, whom she experiences as exerting qualities of strength. This reflects a widespread tendency for Indians to see reflected in themselves what the dominant society describes about them:

> *My husband is a non-Indian and he's more assertive or outgoing, and I think an Indian man would be, seems like an Indian would be more quiet and drawn-in, where he's [my husband] more talkative, communicates more, and he's not shy.* —Diane (Indian patient)

Silence and long pauses, however, are important and positively valued parts of Indian linguistic habitus. Non-Indians find it difficult to recognize and learn this because silence is so often negatively valued in their own society and is experienced as a breakdown in communication between people who are not family or close friends (following Eades, 1994a, p. 242). Indian societies, on the contrary, value silence as a participant's desire to think or enjoy the presence of others in a non-verbal manner, while signifying respect and patience rather than ignorance. These thoughts clearly express this, and in the context of biomedicine, it interferes with clear communications:

Among the people a pause is longer and they're used to having the time, and because the dominant society is more time-oriented, the pauses are shorter. There's a lack of, to our way of thinking, it's a lack of respect to be interrupted when really it's just a matter of differences in culture. Yes, slow down you know. Although people think that we're quiet because we don't know or are dumb or something, it's not that. It's a sign of respect to be quiet and to listen. Young people nowadays they'll do that. High school people, a lot of them, they don't know that. There's so much of our culture that's been lost between the generations, it's sad.
—Hannah (Indian patient)

Sure, I think [silence] is a great virtue in a very socially complicated society and that people, as patients, measure their words. They [Indians] won't say something that they don't mean necessarily, and that may mean that a lot of time they're quiet. It might mean that they'll think it over before they respond or they won't make it up as they go. —Teresa (non-Indian)

Silence is an essential element of showing respect and understanding. The respect one shows to an elder serves to create an area of quietness and receptivity into which the elder can speak. Speaking seems to be created out of an active silence of complete emptiness. This is especially true for elders who have been less influenced by mainstream culture and media exposure. Elders use silence as a sign of respect toward their clinicians, while in the rush of scheduling, they are often perceived as ignorant instead:

*Silence from a person seeing a doctor does not neces-
sarily mean ignorance. It's being polite to give the professional a chance to talk, because he's a professional. He [the
doctor] needs to exercise patience in communication and if
that's not possible with elders, they need to listen and then
have patience.* —Austine (Indian patient)

"Coming-to-knowing" arises out of that silence (Peat, 1994, pp.
68-79). Some Indians, however, love to chat and will talk through
the night. Yet, at the same time, each person has a quality of silence.
The critical factor in the Indian's decision whether to speak or keep
silent lies in the nature of relationships to other people in focused
gatherings or encounters (Basso, 1970, p. 216). There is less silence
when in the company of extended family or close friends in casual
encounters. Keeping silent is also associated with social situations
where participants perceive role expectations or context to be am-
biguous and/or unpredictable. Health care settings are obvious settings where such ambiguities occur both in role and context where
worldviews differ significantly.

Patients who feel vulnerable, perhaps ashamed, and obligated to
keep personal and family concerns private can be assured that information will be kept confidential and reassured that it is often difficult for patients to disclose personal information. Among tightly knit
Indian communities, there is often an unspoken familiarity with the
cause of someone's silence. This patient describes how knowing a
family can explain whether silence is grief or a preference for quiet:

*At times like I know a lot of the families and the events
that might have occurred with those families go with knowing them for a long time, you know. You could almost understand why somebody is experiencing what they're experiencing [silence]. They might have some extreme grief issues, but
I don't see them as sad just because they didn't communicate
with you right off.* —Russell (Indian)

Silence is such an important quality that young Indian children
have been taught to remain silent throughout Indian history. After
winter's first snow, when oral stories are most often told, children

are taught to listen and learn from what they hear. They are not habitually told how to behave by their parents, as are non-Indian children, but are taught to learn lessons by carefully listening to stories and nature and by listening to their elders as this patient explains:

The Natives here have a tendency to really pause. Yes! You'll say something. They'll pause to think about it. I don't know if it's a learned behavior from childhood, because, you know, we are taught to listen and not interrupt since you're little. My grandma even tells us to listen, to observe, to watch and listen. That's how we learn. So I think it is taught to us from a small age. We're to listen and then to think about it and then if we have questions, we can ask. —Vine (Indian patient)

Silence is communicative in other ways as well. For instance, it often substitutes for words in emotionally charged conversations, in delicate situations, in times of grief, or when the topic involves kinship taboos. The Indian patients below describe intricacies and bonds of kinship as they affect talk and silence, particularly in delicate situations:

It depends on relationships—how the extended family is set up, how it works, who talks to who, and who doesn't talk to who. The clan system is very important, and if there is a person or family that your family doesn't talk to, then you don't either. It's just not done. You don't talk. —Wendy (Indian patient)

In the way old days, I wouldn't even be able to talk to my mother-in-law directly. And that's changed over time, but it goes back that far that if I saw that she needed something I couldn't walk up and say, "Hey, Mom, I'll do this for you." We do that now because we've changed, but in the old days I wouldn't talk to her, she wouldn't talk to me. —David (Indian patient)

My brother, he got into a fight with this other guy. Over a girlfriend. They had a big and long fight and now no one of us will talk to any of them and they don't talk to us either. We don't do that. —Russell (Indian)

Silence for both White health clinicians and Indian patients is a way of conveying whether they are attending to the talk of another. But in non-Indian interaction, that silence is often mixed with brief comments such as "yeses" and "mmm hmms" from listeners that serve the same function as head nods to convey that the listener is paying attention. Clinicians experience fewer cues indicating that Indians are attending because Indians nod less and take longer pauses between turns at talk than non-Indians. Thus, even though the average difference between non-Indian and Indian length of pause between turns is quite small, the clinician who just spoke may have to wait longer before receiving a response that may or may not provide evidence that the hearer is attending.

There are longer silences or pauses between speakers' turns at talk. A non-Indian person typically takes a one-second pause between sentences to indicate that the other person is to speak. Indians may wait longer than five seconds between sentences to indicate that they are finished speaking (Tafoya, 1989). This difference may cause the non-Indian to unintentionally cut Indians off before they even begin to speak.

As with many other problems of communicating, the pressure of time is a significant factor that shapes all conversations in the health care system, and it dramatically interferes with Indians' practice of silence. Even five-second pauses are taken as endings, with clinicians filling in the space with further questions, often cutting off the patient's thought process and preempting the next response. Patients are quite aware of time pressures that serve both to hurry their talk and prevent them from speaking what they have on their minds, as expressed in these comments:

I don't think that the system gives them space to wait for a 20-second pause or to attend to people in the way that they would like to be attended to, and I think everybody knows that. I think that that's known to the patients as well. Nobody likes it, but those people [clinicians] are in a rush. I think it would be virtually impossible, given the workload here. I don't know how that would work out. I think they get used to it, but I don't think anybody likes it. I don't think any of us like to be hurried, and so I kind of relate it more to hurrying. —Teresa (non-Indian)

It seems to me that you're in the room, you have 15 minutes or less or more. It's 15 minutes if I'm not mistaken. You're trying to get everything done within that 15 minutes and, say the elders are talking, they might pause. My grandpa does that when he talks, he pauses for long times and the doctor might jump in there and just maybe ask another question before the last question was done. —David (Indian patient)

Gendered silence can occur, however, when there is difficulty in handling questions. Female patients, especially, find it humiliating and painful to share stories and current health problems with a male doctor. Not only does it go against the kinship structure, but it also causes extreme embarrassment and a tendency not to be forthright, as these females discuss:

I'm very modest. I think I'm kind of polite (laugh). Um, I prefer to talk to a woman doctor, which I have asked for if it's for a female health problem or health concern. — Vine (Indian patient)

It's more traditional that a personal preference among most of the females is that we share things, you'd rather have female anyway, especially even among female problems and everything. There is a definite separation of the sexes in those cultures. —Emilie (Indian patient)

In addition to the difficulties of silence and pauses, interruptions, according to Jack Bilmes (1997), are violations of speaking rights, often used to silence stories of history, culture, and lifestyle or health, because they are not understood or found relevant. This is seen in the structure of specific questions, the practice of interrupting, and prompts for how to answer questions. When clinicians at IHS employ these strategies as part of their biomedical training, they are not aware of how much it keeps them from receiving the very information they are seeking from their patients, and they are apt to jump to incorrect conclusions as the next example illustrates:

And we're not quite done thinking about what they said in the first place. Sometimes it just gets overran and it just continues throughout the whole appointment. Maybe they're [doctors] thinking it hasn't been going on that long [the silence], maybe they're not sure it's the correct pain that they have, where it's at. They're probably thinking that you're not sure exactly if you have a pain or not! Are you really sick? So I think they just assume that you're in there because you just have an ache at that moment and you're not quite sure why. —Vine (Indian patient)

During a medical interview, disruption of an Indian patient's narrative is considered rude and inconsiderate. One of the most frequently quoted studies (Beckman & Frankel, 1984) suggests that when physicians ask patients to describe their concerns, they were usually redirected after the first stated concern and after a mean time of only 18 seconds of speaking. Furthermore, in only 1 of 52 visits did patients return to redirect their questions and receive closure about their concerns. Because of this, clinicians often redirected a patient's concern without knowledge of other issues the patient might need to bring forth or whether the pursued concern was even the most important one. Rather than using the term interruption to describe this behavior, some linguists feel that "redirection" more clearly indicates verbal intercessions that aim the focus of the interview before patients are able to complete initial accounts of their concerns. A clinician admits her tendency to redirect conversations, and a patient expresses her frustration:

[I start to get impatient], then you tend to jump in and cut them off and give them words. —Sapphire (non-Indian clinician)

I don't like them [interruptions]. [It makes me feel] that I'm a hypochondriac or something to that effect. Because they assume they know more about my condition than I do [and] that they think they know about my condition. And it's also not a safe assumption to make because everyone who has my condition is different, has differences, different things. —Austine (Indian patient)

The following are thoughts and advice that might be more help-ful for doctors to understand and deal with patient silences and interruptions:

Be still, wait until people are finished before asking an-other question [interrupting], be sure that they have said what they want to say, watch, take in everything with your eyes, that's a way of listening too, listen to the whole per-son, remember. —Teresa (non-Indian)

Interruptions and redirections are a common reflection of differ-ent cultures as well as the real restraints of time and how much can be accomplished in a session. The negative value of silence has been analyzed, especially when it is being misinterpreted and misjudged by non-Indians in reference to fast and slow talkers (Tannen & Saville-Troike, 1985a). Fast talkers are associated with interrupting and upsetting others. But fast talkers can also feel uncomfortable because the speech of slow talkers is punctuated with pauses, which fast talkers experience as rude silences that break the pace of con-versation. Conversation is a process of taking turns and can be dis-rupted when cross-cultural participants are unaccustomed to the other's worldview and use of silence.

IHS clinicians are trained in the culture of biomedicine to be fast talkers, and to get information quickly, to ask rapid questions, and move on to the next patient. Thus, speakers who are perceived to have the most power usually control conversation direction: clini-cians. Because silencing is used so that the clinician can resume talk-ing or reduce patient responses to short answers, it often interrupts the patients' narrative to say what they want and in their own words. This prevents patients from talking about their health problems, as this individual illustrates:

So they're [Indians] not quite so willing ad libbers. Oh, I think that [clinicians] in a hurry often run over [your talk].

*I just consider it to be a special brand of rudeness. It's just
something. I certainly tolerate it and understand it, but I
think that you will find things like that in a medical situation
because those [clinicians] are operating on a terrific schedule. The other thing is when you're in a situation when docs
always assume that they know more than you do, and maybe
they do, I don't know, but if they're sure of that, well then
they're sure of your response before you respond, and so
they will run over you and they do.* —Teresa (non-Indian)

Thus, even though the average difference between the Indian
and non-Indian length of a pause between turns is quite small, it is
still the case that the person who just spoke must wait longer before
receiving a response that may or may not provide evidence in the
auditory channel that the hearer is attending. Though narrative may
be preferred by most patients, time constraints often do not allow for
the luxury of silence. Tafoya has suggested that the use of indirect
forms of questioning and waiting for a response are the best forms
of communication of information gathering, and conversely that Indians typically expect professionals to take a directive role (1989, p.
316).

*I think the doctors here have to learn the culture and
really take the time, and they're the ones that should really
be asking more questions with the patients or first learn
who they are, their family.* —Vine (Indian patient)

There is an uneasy balance between narrative information and
directive questions. Brucker cites several studies that reveal how directive styles are more effective for patients than professionals who
use nondirective styles, and that the ethnicity of the health professional may not be as important as culturally appropriate training
methods for understanding Indian communicative patterns of silence and how it impacts trust (1998, p. 316).

Silence and silencing also have to do with perceptions and functions of the power/dominance spectrum that exists between mainstream Westernized societies and marginal societies such as tribal
communities. Languages are not neutral vehicles for the transmission of thoughts. Instead, languages are imbedded in the history and

struggles of the people who use them. Silence can disturb and disrupt the linguistic hegemony that is inherent in and coalesces the power relations between the dominant majority and communities of power (Montoya, 2000). There is sometimes an ambivalent relationship toward the power that clinicians hold, which results in an unusual combination of both mistrust and respect for authority. The following patient anticipates how clinicians respond to Indian silence:

> *I would presume they are figuring either this person doesn't trust me or doesn't think I'm a good doctor or doesn't really want to be here, and that really isn't the case. People go there because they're hurt, because they're sick and they do want the treatment, but at the same time they're not going to react the same way.* —David (Indian patient)

Because few doctors have had any cultural training about the tribe or clan structures in which they begin to work, they often have pan-Indian concepts that pertain to stereotypical notions of what an Indian is. Due also to the long history of forced assimilation, removal from their lands, government policies, court decisions, and the small percentage of their minority population, Indians are one of the most powerless social groups. Culturally appropriate relationships may need to be built that cross boundaries of habitus before silences may be overcome. Silence is often negatively valued by doctors and frequently interpreted as an indication of some kind of communication breakdown that results in potential lapses of proper care.

Indians can also use silence to circumvent clinic rules and control, and still retain the medical attention and resources they desire. Such cultural performances as patients are important resources in obtaining resources controlled by experts, (medicines, drugs, etc.). Some patients seem to display skepticism when submitted to questioning and wonder whether the doctors are tricksters who conceal their lack of knowledge by asking many questions—a familiar trait of Indian tricksters. There are also times when silence is a means of keeping from boasting about oneself and drawing personal attention, as this patient reveals:

Silence is a good tool, so you need to be comfortable with it. Personally, to get something out of [people], they're not going to share. In fact, sometimes it's rude to share, especially with someone who knows more than you do. So they are not necessarily going to tell you, and some of that is cultural, but some of it is also is an esteem issue. It isn't really, it's not okay to beat your own drum and put yourself out there, whereas in the White world that would be more comfortable. That's not, it's a tribal thing. —Emilie (Indian patient)

Silence, though hardly noticed by many non-Indian people, is thus a constant source of conversation interference. Not only does it prevent patients from thinking, but also clinicians use silence as an invitation to interrupt, redirect conversations, and misinterpret important medical information. Time constraints only add to the tendency to widen the abyss between clinicians and their Indian patients.

My field notes revealed that, although I trained myself to be theoretically and practically knowledgeable about silence and pauses, I found it difficult to readily be patient, especially during the first few interviews. Once again, my language style identified more with fast-talking Indian clinicians who have difficulty in dealing with their patients' silences and long pauses:

•Though the interview process went smoothly, stories were told, and questions were asked and addressed, there were longer pauses than I am used to. I was glad I knew enough to patiently wait, *some* of the time. I know from my own family and academic experiences that I am a fast talker, used to fighting for the floor, and aggressively asserting myself. I find through these interviews that I typically and continuously tend to interrupt and redirect the conversation much more than I had previously been aware of. I experienced quite an amount of frustration with myself for not being able to refrain from this behavior as much as I tried. Though I succeeded more than I first thought I could, I felt I failed miserably in preventing myself from doing so altogether or even most of the time, especially in the beginning.

•I thought to myself, "If I can't do this, when I am fully cognizant of the issue and my own struggle to refrain from interrupting and allowing long silences, then how can other non-Indians or clinicians new to reservation health care settings expect to do any better to change their own tendency to do the same?" I found myself apologizing frequently for cutting people off and shaking my head at my own failures. There were obvious times where my interruptions caused the conversation to deteriorate.

•I had more of a problem with interrupting than with waiting through long pauses. I did not experience the pauses as uncomfortable, however, and actually found it surprisingly pleasant as I went through more and more interviews to take a slower pace than I was used to. I was also amazed, in spite of my previous knowledge, at how seldom small children interrupted conversations. Surprisingly, hardly anyone let on that they were distressed by my interruptions, though I thought they should have been.

Confidentiality, Gossip, Gender, and Trust

Maintaining silence as clinicians for the sake of confidentiality is one of their most important role activities, since trust is a vital component of the therapeutic relationship. Patients who trust their clinicians will feel confident that clinicians will also reciprocate with respect for the patient's right to privacy and confidentiality. Patients will feel more comfortable discussing their symptoms and disclosing intimate details of their lives (Gumperz & Levinson, 1996, p. 195). This patient suggests that sincerity of care is an ingredient of building trust:

If you're sincere, they know it and then they trust you and especially if they think this is going to help them get better or get some help, then they will open up. —Quail (Indian patient/clinician)

As Foucault theorized, doctor-patient discourse may reveal status and power differences. Such differences are reflected in the ways intonation and stress are employed, the way questions are asked by the clinician, or the ways doctors perceive questions from the patient. The office, clinic, or hospital seems to make many patients feel uncomfortable. Trust is a vital component of the health care relationship. Patients who feel trust with their clinicians will feel confident that their clinicians will watch after their best interests and that they will also respect patients' right to privacy and confidentiality (Luckmann, 2000, p. 126). A breach of this trust will cause a patient to refrain from seeing a particular clinician and to choose another, as this Indian patient has chosen to do:

I think that this one nurse talks about what goes on here on the outside. I choose not to see her at all. It's not [kept] confidential, so I just tell them that too, that it's not confidential, so I don't want to see her. I just tell them right there at the front desk. —Gertrude (Indian patient)

Because of lapses of confidentiality, Indian patients will also feel uncomfortable discussing their symptoms or disclosing intimate details of their lives to IHS clinicians. The nature of the close-knit Indian community will also influence how many personal details a patient is willing to share with care providers, in fear that everybody will know their business. This Indian patient clearly illustrates the point:

That's one thing I don't feel comfortable with at IHS, I don't know, people, like people know you at that place because you've grown up around there and stuff and people kinda gossip really bad, too. So, like if I had to go to the doctor for something personal, I wouldn't go to IHS, like I prefer to go to, you know, to like one of the clinics up here where you can be like more anonymous and stuff 'cause I don't trust the privacy of IHS. 'Cause I used to be really good friends with some of the people who work there, and they would tell me other people's business, like other people what they were in the doctor for and stuff, and that's what made me really weary of going there, like when I found out I was pregnant, I wasn't ready to tell my family yet, so I didn't go there because I knew if I went there, I knew that

*everybody in the community would know before I had a
chance to tell my parents and stuff. I just didn't feel comfortable with it.* —Carla (Indian patient)

The clinician is often constrained by the bureaucratic work environment (Gumperz & Levinson, 1996, pp. 195-196) of government health care contexts such as IHS. The language employed not
only reflects the clinician's training and the desire to be accurate and
concise, but also a professional image and status among patients and
other professionals. This Indian female discloses her willingness to
see a male doctor based on experiences of respecting male relatives
and expectations of professional behavior:

*[Earlier on] there were very few women [clinicians] and
I personally have never had a woman doctor, even for OB-
GYN. And I trust them explicitly, very professional, and although this is a matriarchal society, men were warriors and
men are valued. I have a lot of brothers and a lot of uncles.
So I just have great respect for men, and I trust them. Luckily
I've not had any bad experiences with men, I feel very pro-
tected. They have a special place, so it's easier for us to accept that the doctor, the male doctor and his status, and you
trust him and you expect him to be a man.* —Quail (Indian
patient/clinician)

Clinicians and patients clearly are not exempt from the tragedy
of failing to understand one another or even themselves. The impact
of such communicative failures that lead to a breakdown of trust
with health encounters contradicts one of the most basic and revered
professional dogmas: that clinicians can be totally trusted because
they act "only in their patients' best interests." This dogma only
compounds the tragedy by assuming an identity of interests and
brushing aside the necessity of clarifying differences in expectations and objectives. A thorough knowledge of patients and their
family backgrounds helps to build trust, but in IHS settings, such
continuity of care is often lacking. Concluding his famous lecture
on "The Care of the Patient," Francis Peabody (1988 [1976], p. 545)
movingly spoke: "The good physician knows his patients through
and through, and his knowledge is bought dearly. Time, sympathy,

and understanding must be lavishly dispensed, but the reward is to be found in that personal bond which forms the greatest satisfaction of the practice of medicine. One of the essential qualities of the clinician is interest in humanity, for the secret of the care of the patient is caring for the patient."

If "interest in humanity" is an essential professional quality, and if it defines the art of medicine, it must be taught and learned as thoroughly as bioscience is being taught. Above all, clinicians and patients must learn to converse competently with one another. Meaningful conversation, however, requires that they trust each other. Powerful cultural obstacles stand in the path of trust and conversation. Breaches of confidence in the face of clinicians' role of power contribute to mistrust in medical interviews:

> *There's trust issues. Yeah, no wonder I feel hesitant to come in and tell you about myself when this and that happened to so and so, and we all know about it, heard about it from [the clinic].* —Wendy (Indian patient)

Trust can alternatively serve to prevent patients from being aggressive in talking about their health because they are unable to aggressively go against what they feel is the clinician's power and "all-knowing" abilities to second-guess the patient's agenda, as described:

> *They're not that assertive because they're not that comfortable, and they trust the doctor, they don't question the doctor at all.* —Emilie (Indian patient)

Until recent years, there hasn't been adequate attention focused on the harm caused by causal talk about patients in public spaces, such as elevators or lunchrooms. With such knowledge available, more effort is being made to be considerate of patient privacy.

The non-Indian clinicians below comment on difficulties of maintaining patient privacy on close-knit reservations in social contexts:

> *Because I don't actually live on the rez, I don't know about the talk. I've heard that there's a few that do too much*

talking, employees that do too much talking. I think that's why I'm requested sometime, because they know I'm not going to say anything. I've got young girls that will ask for me because they think that they may have an STD or something and they know I'm not going to say anything. I don't go to [local entertainment], so it's not my personality. And even with my family, I don't say anything. I've made sure, like new patients, if they're friends with my kids or in school with my kids or if they're like my husband [community sponsor], I make sure they know I'm not going to say anything. I know for sure there's one Native nurse, and she takes just as much care into that confidentiality, but the techs, I'm not so sure of, so I'm careful what I tell them sometimes. —Lynn (non-Indian clinician)

I think that's something that could be part of this training is getting it through to people. Now the interesting part about that though, that it isn't always the outsiders [non-Indian clinicians] that are causing that trouble. Well, they're more professionally trained to that confidentiality. So confidentiality is an issue, but then that can be dealt with inside of the medical community as well. And it's a really tough thing. It gets very awkward for me, because I have people come up to me at church, and they'll start talking to me and I say, whoa, you're talking to me about something and you're assuming that I know what you're talking about, but I don't because my husband [who is also a professional on the reservation] doesn't say word one. And he does that because he cares about you and he cares about me, so I don't know what you're talking about. And they'll look at me kind of funny and I say, it's true. And I say if you want to tell me, then I know. But if you don't tell me, then I don't know. But that is an issue and that's the issue of a tight community and of training. —Teresa (Indian patient)

The continuous interactions with and presence of many extended family members on reservations can be confusing in the process of building trust and maintaining confidences when private matters are involved in their health care. There is confusion for clinicians about how to treat family members who are present when it comes to discussing private information about the patient, as this clinician describes:

> *The extended family members, we don't necessarily call them extended family, they're all family, and confidentiality is a big issue. For instance, my brother didn't understand what they were testing him for. I would want to know, and I would want to have access to that doctor and I would want him to explain it to me so I could explain it to my brother. But because of the new whatever privacy thing [HIPAA: Health Insurance Portability and Accountability Act [64]], that's not possible.* —Austine (Indian patient)

Another clinician is frustrated by privacy measures that apply more to mainstream conditions than situations at IHS where extended family members are present most of the time with the patient:

> *Oh, confidentiality problems [are huge], because technically you're not supposed to, you have to very careful what you say. Even with the privacy laws, they were saying you should actually get everybody to sign, and get her to sign that all these [extended family] present can listen to what you're going to say. And that's not going to happen. Everything's just, like it compounds everything.* —Sapphire (non-Indian clinician)

Clinicians will sometimes gossip amongst each other about their patients to relieve stress or gain other viewpoints. Gossiping provides a channel through which people can pass their judgments and opinions about others and their actions. In addition to gossip, however, is the awareness in the community of who the clinicians are, so that if a clinician pays a visit to a home, all the neighbors and family members are aware of it. When it is necessary to make a home visit, confidentiality is also at risk, as the non-Indian clinician

---

[64] HIPAA rules for patient privacy are especially complicated when dealing with tribal families and clan/kin members who show up at appointments with the patient.

below reports. She also describes how many Indians will feel more trusting of a non-Indian who may not be directly involved in reservation gossip:

> *Sometimes they don't like talking to a rez person because of how they're related to them or, maybe, it's usually more like they're kind of related to them in a certain way, and they want it more confidential, then they [non-Indians] may come in more handy. If [gossip gets around] and it does, I think it's more like, if you go see [patients], you kind of give it away. Like, what was [the clinician] at so and so's house for, it's probably because they have something or other. It's that way, and also I think it's sometimes the patient. But then we've also had documented medical breaches of medical records where patients have. . . .* —Sapphire (non-Indian clinician)

> *I think doctors gossip, but here I don't think it's so much the doctors, because the doctors don't know the community, don't visit among the community. It has to be people from here. It comes up quite regularly. It doesn't change. I don't know how you'd do it short of firing all the locals, which you don't want to do because IHS is one of the main employment institutions on the reservation.* —Hannah (Indian patient)

Thus, gossip works in two directions: creating a kind of "alliance: between gossipers and enabling them to reflect about themselves in relation to others" by "measuring who's up who's down" (Spacks, 1985, p. 5). Gossip can function to create rapport, intimacy and involvement on one hand, and at the same time it can reveal judgments about the patients being talked about.

Non-Indians refer to the difficulty of maintaining private information in the record-keeping process or problems with patients who are reluctant to provide information that they know will be written in their charts for a variety of clinicians to read:

> *I'm sure record keeping must be really important, but we don't want some of the things they need to know in the records, so you're not going tell those things. So if you don't*

know them, it's not the doctor's fault all the time. But truth-
fully, if I have some of these problems, I don't want it written
if I know everybody in the staff is going to be able to read
that file either. So we're just going to ignore that and that's
probably the real problem. So I'm going to have this other
little thing here to try to get what I think I need. There's go-
ing to be secrets. And they don't get to the point. It may take
two or three visits to get to the point. And the fact that's okay,
if you tell me this it is not going to be written down in your
record. Maybe we could keep a little separate journal on you
or something. They don't want their whole story out there.
—Teresa (Indian patient)

Closely related to issues of confidentiality and privacy within
the structure of kinship systems is the comfort or discomfort of gender relationships, as was discussed in the section on kinship behavior and taboos. It is common for Indian homes to include multigen-
erational families. Families may also include members identifying
with to up to four variants of gender, unlike the traditional non-Indian references of male and female. "Two-spirited"[65] is the term
currently used to express the distinct Indian approach to gender
identity. Two-spirit individuals have valued roles in the community
and kinship systems. Generational and gender roles are fluid, accepted, and expressed. It is often seen as a gift to be two-spirited but
an anomaly to non-Indian clinicians.

"As an American Indian and a scholar, I know that In-
dian cultures have endured because we have held on to the
positive values that allowed us to overcome hardship. I also
know that those same values will allow us to not only survive,
but thrive, in the future. But in order to do so, we must in-
sure that no person is excluded. When we lose even one in-
dividual, we are weaker.

---

[65] The term "two-spirit" came in to use during the third annual intertribal Native
American/First Nations gay and lesbian conference in Winnipeg, Canada, 1990.

Our ancestors would not recognize the term "LGBT" (lesbian, gay, bisexual, transgender), but "two-spirit" people were (and are) respected as healers, artisans, wives, husbands, and holy people. Another term that our ancestors would not know is "domestic partnerships for same-sex couples," but Native people respected the path the Creator set each of us in our journey and accepted when two individuals chose each other as life mates.

Our world is fragile. We need our relatives near us. Let us embrace them, not push them away."[66] —Walter Fleming, Kickapoo; Department Chair of Native American Studies, Montana State University.

When it comes to health care, such gender identifications and boundaries bring forth complications when personal issues of body and health are concerned—not just privacy of words but of bodies. What is revealed is tied into silence and gaze and more pronounced traditional values of physical privacy (modesty) than is common in non-Indian cultures. This non-Indian clinician explains the role of modesty and undressing, especially when with the opposite gender:

Nobody gets undressed, male or female. Not for any type of exam, unless you ask them specifically, I need to see this portion, then it's not going to be revealed to you, male or female. We probably still have the original dressing gowns that we bought . . . never been touched since we bought them. The women for the most part as far as OB-GYN kind of stuff and breast exams usually go to the female providers. We [male clinicians] offer to take care of you. If you don't want to, that's okay by me. I'm not offended if you won't let me examine you. It needs to be examined and I strongly urge you to get this taken care of. If you want me to do it, fine, we'll get it taken care of right now. We'll get it done. Or schedule an appointment with one of the female providers. They schedule an appointment with a female provider. The men have no problem. If I need to check the prostate, but

---

[66]"Fair is Fair in Montana" (fairisfairmontana.org), August 12, 2012, retrieved September 1, 2016.

they wouldn't go to a female doctor. —Evan (non-Indian clinician)

This individual relates her Foucauldian feelings of being just a physiological location under the clinician's gaze, who is not seen as a human with dignity or a sense of modesty:

It is like a deference to people's sensitivities about their lives and bodies. You want somebody to understand that you don't like being a hunk of meat on the table. —Teresa (Indian patient)

Clinicians sometimes leave the room with patients left undressed and exposed. Indian patients especially experience this as a lack of respect, vulnerability, and a source of great distress, both personal and social. This patient gives excellent details of such situations:

I went to the specialist. Well, he left me on this table and proceeded to see two or three other people before he come in. He left me there exposed. And I remember, because there I was stuck on the table and the only thing I could see, and I looked down and I saw these incredible Italian leather shoes that he was wearing, and I still remember those shoes. And I thought about it, I thought there was a relationship between those shoes and the obtuse comment, the question that he'd asked me. I looked at that and I said, Well, thanks a lot," and I left. —Teresa (non-Indian)

Connected to such personal and social feelings of modesty and trust are power, fear, shame, and being judged about one's own body and health problems. This patient clearly relates her feeling of being judged:

Sometimes it's embarrassing because you feel vulnerable. Most of us only like to take our clothes off under certain circumstances and we don't like it under other circumstances. That's the truth and so most of us I think, too, after the fear factor comes the shame factor, I think a lot of us have come to feel pretty bad about our bodies in a lot of ways partly because we don't stay in good shape and maybe because people have been insensitive. You know you really ought to lose weight. You feel that way, but then you go do it. You look pretty good to me, but good enough is kind of not good enough when you go to the doctors because you assume that they're going to be judgmental. Whether they are or not, they could be the nicest person in the world, but you still know that they are looking for healthy bodies and you haven't got one. I don't know if that's true of everybody. Some people don't care a bit, but I know for me, that I sure feel that way. So I just plum stay away as much as I can. If I can take care of myself some other way, I will. —Teresa (non-Indian)

Because of kinship behaviors and restrictions, matters of privacy and modesty, many more Indian patients than non-Indian patients prefer gendered communications with clinicians who do not cross kinship boundaries or taboos. Many females interviewed preferred female clinicians for both general and private examinations. Such preferences were strongly voiced about their fervent sense of modesty, privacy, the separation of sexes, female exams, and most of them request female doctors. Likewise, men reported that they prefer male clinicians in order to more comfortably speak about impotence, prostate cancer, and sexually transmitted diseases.

This comment confirms the role of confidence for same gender preference, with explicit reference to being touched on the body by another gender. Some patients will absolutely avoid crossing the gender line in any way if an examination involves being touched, which is experienced as inappropriate:

We request, if something has gone wrong, we request a woman doctor. I would not go ahead with a male doctor— don't mind having a man doctor, but if he's going to do anything to my body, it's got to be a woman doctor. And that's what everybody likes; they don't like men doctors touching parts that they don't . . . —Karen (Indian patient)

Gender differences and prejudices were also revealed differently in this comment:

The odd part is that there are all kinds of prejudices that come into play. One of them being that a lot of people would prefer a guy simply because they assume there's greater competence there. And that would be true whether it's male or female as a patient—not so much that they're smarter, but they assume, their stereotype is that a good doctor is a man, so then they'll want one, he or she. And then if they don't have that attitude, well then they won't care. I think that's changing and most women have been able to get into that position, and it takes time. I've seen one that didn't do so well that way, and I've seen several that did just fine, and then I've seen a couple of women where they just were insisting that [female clinicians] were quacks, and I thought, well I don't know about that. So that kind of varied a lot, having to do with confidence and experience and personality and things like that. —Teresa (non-Indian)*

Varying levels of confidentiality, privacy, gossip, modesty, and gender preference all add to Indian patients' discomfort with interaction, trust, and disclosing health information at IHS facilities. Medical and community relationships are references that should be taken seriously in guarding patient privacy in order to allow patients to bring forward their health concerns. If patients do not experience such safety, their health will be immeasurably affected for the worse. If biomedical training and procedures ignore these crucial aspects of Indian worldview, the gulf between cultures and health care will continue to increase.

I had fewer field notes in reference to confidentiality as a topic, since I addressed my own concerns about interviewing confidentiality so thoroughly beforehand. Because gossip came up spontaneously during the interviews, I made a note that prompted me to add the topic to this inquiry in connection with confidentiality. The following field notes address these topics:

•When she told me she would rather pay to see a private doctor that she couldn't afford rather than go to the IHS clinic, I realized how much of a problem gossip is. It is not just that everybody's business gets spread around the tight-knit reservation population, but to avoid this, she wouldn't even go get help if she needed it. Then gossip transforms from invasion of privacy and modesty to actively preventing people from seeking health care for their problems. Unlike gender issues, where she could ask for a female doctor, gossip makes her want to avoid the entire health system altogether. This is a serious interference. She knows it is not the doctors who talk but the Indian workers who are all connected to everyone on the reservation through multiple kinship ties. She doesn't like her business getting home before she does. I don't blame her. Because of the ramifications of this, I think this is worth bringing up in the findings of this inquiry.

•Another woman was upset about having to see the doctor and ashamed of her body, thinking [the doctor] was disgusted with her. She didn't want to be there and thought she wouldn't come back again. She hates the idea of having her chart and her business passed around from person to person and department to department. She assumes people typically read what's in it and talk in the lunch room or elevators. I know how much it would bother me if I felt that way (and maybe I should be more upset and concerned, now that I think of it, and since I've also witnessed the same phenomena in elevators). Her lack of trust makes her feel powerless about her own health and ashamed of her body and its needs.

•Sometimes she [a clinician] says she doesn't want to call or visit someone because everyone else at the home and neighborhood will know what it's about. She tries to find ways to tell him privately but says sometimes there is no way, and she does the best she can. When she answers her office phone, I can see that she deliberately doesn't want to say anything using a name or personal information in front of me, and I see that she really is aware of respecting the patient's privacy. When I mention this to her, she says she wishes other staff did the same, and that maybe because some of the staff lives here, it's more tempting to talk about people they know. She knows the problem exists but doesn't know why people keep gossiping when it hurts their own reputation. Maybe, she says, gossip is more important and people get used to it. I don't know. I'll have to see if I can find out more about it. I know it would affect me if I knew people were gossiping about me in my doctor's office. I assume they don't, but maybe that's naïve. Even to have such assumptions is naïve as well.

Non-Indian clinicians are not only highly educated in the academy but also commonly regarded as all-knowing, godlike, actively verbal, and often arrogant—regardless of the ethnicity of the patient. The ambiguity between power and trust is a tricky one, regardless of gender. IHS clinicians that are perceived as well educated, upper class, and knowledgeable authorities often fulfill this stereotype:

> *This is a two-way education process, because in the White world we understand perfectly well what the exchange is between them, whether we like it or not. We know that we're going to go there, the doctor is God, you better ask him, treat him like God, and he'll give you a good deal. If you want to be a difficult patient or whatever, who knows what you're going to get? It's a double education process so maybe the ideal place would be to have the spiritual person or have the shaman do the intake. There's only so much, whatever, there's only so much you can do. I personally don't expect my doctor to do everything, but if he listens to me and does whatever, if I need something I tell him, here's what I need. You gotta learn to play this system. I'll treat you like God, and you give me what I want. Okay fine.*
> —Emilie (Indian patient)

> *So they need to be educated in the culture pretty much. And it doesn't mean that they have to immerse in it. Just the fact that things are different here, you're in a foreign country. [It's important to have] respect for the elders, respect for all the patients, and most all of them are like that pretty much. There's a few that they think they're God's gift to medicine.* —David (Indian patient)

> *IHS has such a high turnover of medical staff. I think all physicians at some point or another has the God complex.*
> —Hannah (Indian patient)

Probably it's a lot like the 1950s and 60s approach to physicians, they're all-knowing and whatever you say, doc, I'll do, no questions asked. I suppose the more enlightened consumer now questions your every move. —Evan (non-Indian clinician)

I heard a doctor one time years ago. I used to work [on another reservation]. I was there for five years. I got along well with him. He was a good doctor and he made a comment that I never forgot because I thought, really, you miss the mark in what you're doing here, and he had come back to our little area, and he had done something, I don't remember what it had to do with, but he said, "I want to get back and see my patients, I can't let them see me like this. They see me as being infallible, like the Pope," he says, you know. And that really got to me. —Peace (Indian patient)

Whether doctors are seen as God or not, it is true that a failure to respond cannot automatically be taken as evidence of miscomprehension; but in practice, that inference is made (Philips, 1983, p. 96). Though some patients may continue to be guarded and silent in fear of being discriminated against, dominated, or misunderstood, it can be best for the doctor to wait for the patient to defer questions to a later time when trust has been established through a growing and long-term relationship that comes with continuity of care. The frequent turnover of doctors at the IHS facilities, who often agree to work to pay off medical school loans, is a barrier to such long-term continuity and trust unless a purposeful effort on their part is made. The following patient clearly elucidates the conflicts between the art of relating and the lack of personal continuity as contributing to poor IHS health communications:

Connecting with people, having the ability to relate to people is an art more than a profession. I don't think all the training in the world is going to help you communicate with people if you just don't have that natural ability to relate to people, which includes empathy, respect, regard for the people that you work with. Leading up to that incident, the situation that I had, years ago, I worked in a different tribe.

I'd been there for about a year, little over a year, and one of the local men I was working with as a patient came to me. He said I want to ask you something. I said fine if I can answer, I will. He said how long are you going to stay here, and I said I don't know. I didn't set any time limits on how long I'm going to be here. Then I asked him, "Why do you ask me?" I put it politely. And he said, "Well I'll tell you why." He said, "We have a lot of people come through here, some stay for a year, some longer," he said. But the reason I ask you this, some people come here, and we know that they're just spending time. But some come here and work with us, work amongst us, work for us, and we begin to like them and respect them, but then they have to leave. And he said, "Are you going to do that to us?" And I said, "I don't have plans to." So that's really important. —Peace (Indian patient)*

The following advice for getting around the problem of frequent clinical rotations in order to provide a sense of continuity and trust for IHS patients is so simple, yet almost impossible:

Maybe it would be helpful to get some trusted person or somebody that was really good to do a pre-interview with people, so they could listen to the whole story, make a few notes, and get a little bit of the background and a little bit of the story. —Teresa (non-Indian)

5
NONVERBAL MISCOMMUNICATIONS

Many people consider language, in some fundamental sense, to be a spoken or verbal phenomenon. However, there are written languages and languages that depend on hand shapes, signing, body language, or other visual clues for the presentation of meaning. Some of these communications may have been derived from spoken language traditions at particular times, but all of them are fully developed linguistic systems in their own right, whose rules of grammar and discourse may or may not be similar to the grammars and discourses of the spoken languages with which they may be associated (Leap, 1993, p. 6).

A basic finding of sociolinguistics is that, although both language and language usage are structured, it is the latter which responds most sensitively to extra-linguistic influences (Hymes, 1962, 1964; Ervin-Tripp, 1964, 1967; Gumperz, 1964; and Slobin, 1967). A number of studies have addressed the problem of how factors in the social environment of speech events delimit the range and condition the selection of message forms. There is considerable evidence to suggest that extra-linguistic factors influence not only the use of speech but its actual occurrence as well (Basso, 1970, p. 69).

Extra-linguistic (or nonverbal) communication refers to the information transmitted from speakers to listeners when the dominant meaning is not conveyed by words (Zeuschner, 1997, p. 80). Extra-linguistic communication is a multi-channeled process that usually is performed spontaneously, typically involving a subtle set of nonverbal behaviors that often are enacted subconsciously (Lustig & Koester, 1999, p. 205). Nonverbal and verbal communications are entwined as active roles in communication (Goffman, 1981; Hall, 1990; Knapp, 1972; and Labov, 1964).

Nonverbal communication can include many distinctive sets of behavior, including eye behavior, touching behavior, proxemics, and time. Just because these characteristics act outside verbal communication, does not imply that they are unimportant or universally understood, though they are more closely linked than verbal behavior (Hall, 1990, pp. vii-viii). It is essential that people understand bodily behavior and not just words, because they are often enacted subconsciously (Hall, 1990, p. x; and Knapp, 1972, p. 184) and culturally acquired as an essential part of social interaction and linguistic habitus.

The clinician-patient relationship is built through communication and the effective use of language. Along with clinical reasoning and observations, nonverbal cues, joined with the skillful use of language, endow clinical power and establish the medical interview as the clinician's most powerful tool (Hampton, Harrison, et al., 1975; Lipkin, 1994; Lipkin, Quill, et al., 1984; and Sandler, 1980).

Research has linked clinicians' communication styles to patients' satisfaction with health care (Buller & Buller, 1987). The patient's satisfaction with clinicians and medical treatment has emerged as an important determinant of compliance (Korsch, Gozzi, et al., 1968; Korsch & Negrete, 1981; and Woolley, Kane, Hughes & Wright, 1978) and appears to be largely a result of the clinician's verbal and nonverbal communication while interacting with the patient (Daly & Hulka, 1975; Korsch, Gozzi, et al., and 1968; Spiro & Heidrich, 1983).

The clinician should not only acquire knowledge and skill, (Luban-Plozza, 1995), but also be the person who listens to and receives non-verbal messages conveyed by the body. Frequently, nevertheless, the untrained clinician may ignore or fail to see certain scarcely obvious, but noteworthy, events during the consultation. When Indian patients communicate in a discreet manner that is different than their non-Indian clinicians, more often than not their nonverbal cues are unrecognized, misinterpreted, and influence the clinician's understanding of the patient and what the patient is trying to communicate.

Clinicians in IHS health settings must be particularly aware of nonverbal differences that occur in Indian communicative styles in order to prevent misdiagnosis and improper treatment. Nonverbal cues are an integral part of Indian language habitus, much more so than in mainstream society. Clinicians who are new to IHS facilities would benefit from awareness of such potential barriers as differences in eye contact, touch, proximity, and time. Time has been an important component of all aspects of this interrogation, woven through the narratives, and will serve to tie together communicative information as a whole.

Eye Contact

The exchange of words and eye gaze between individuals in each other's presence is a very common social arrangement, yet it is one whose distinctive communicative properties are difficult to disentangle. Though body language and visual clues present meaning, "they are fully developed linguistic systems in their own right, whose rules of grammar and discourse may or may not be similar to the grammars and discourses of the spoken languages with which they may be associated" (Leap, 1993, p. 6).

The information individuals provide, whether they send it or exude it, may be embodied or disembodied. A frown, a spoken word, or a kick is a message that senders convey by means of their own current bodily activity, the transmission occurring only during the time that their body is present to sustain this activity (Goffman, 1963, pp. 13-14). The information gathered by the eyes as contrasted with the ears has not been precisely calculated (Hall, 1969, p. 42) through empirical study. This is an area ripe for further research.

Sight begins to take on an added and special role. Individuals can see that they are being experienced in some way, and they will guide at least some of their conduct according to the perceived identity and initial response of their audience. Further, they can be seen to be seeing this, and can see that they have been seen seeing this. Few verbal messages are transmitted without some manner of nonverbal message involved. Conversations are managed through eye movement and eye contact.

When listening to a person speak, nonverbal actions transmit messages, perhaps messages of belief or disbelief of the speaker's thoughts (Lustig & Koester, 1999, p. 206). Both verbal and nonverbal behaviors assume roles in an act of communication. This behavior is enacted differently according to contexts of cultural and social habitus and is embedded in the linguistic habitus of the speakers. Mainstream American speakers regularly maintain direct eye contact and perceive those who don't reciprocate as uninterested or evasive. During health consultations, the subtle business of eye contact can cause false assumptions of the Indian patient's behavior. Therefore, it is necessary to define various roles eye contact plays for both Indians and non-Indians when talking about health problems. It is also important to recognize that the impersonal biomedical gaze belongs to a Western habitus that Indians likely do not share. This non-Indian clinician has learned over the years to understand the difference:

That they don't have direct eye contact, and it's like they're still thinking when they're not looking at you and talking to you. I think that's a sign of respect. It's disrespectful to look you straight in the eye. To me, I think I remember it probably with everybody, but the males may look at you more. It depends, probably the younger ones don't. Well, I've had other health care providers say that bothers them because they're used to looking at you and having you look back. I think part of it is they don't think you're real serious about what you're there for or you're not paying attention to what they are trying to tell you. Some people might feel a little uncomfortable, too, because they think it's not really disrespectful but more like spacey, not paying attention, or they don't care what you're saying. —Sapphire (non-Indian clinician)*

Normally eyes function as the receivers of visual information. Eyes are used to see what is happening in the surroundings. But eyes also are important transmitters of signals that play a role in everyday social interactions (Klopf, 1991, p. 189). When conversing with others, how eyes are looked at and looked away from can make the difference between a successful encounter or an embarrassing one. Gazing lovingly at someone or staring in a hostile manner may be an unconscious action. This example explains how the minimal use of Indian eye contact has been a trained behavior to show respect:

I don't think anybody likes an aggressive bearing, and I think a lot of people don't like exposure in public, so there is a reticence there that's real. Well, if you're put on the spot, not exactly staring you down but buttonholing you, you tend to recede and your eyes will drop and whatnot. I think [young people] have been trained to what they would call respect. And that means that there's a subtlety to their communication visually, and that means that they may not be quite as forward with their eyes, so to speak, unless they're at ease or perceive that that's what they should be doing. You'll find a subtlety of communication. —Teresa (non-Indian)

Speaking from a Western worldview, Kendon (1967) has distinguished roles of eye contact: (1) *Seeking Feedback.* People engage in eye contact more often when they are listening, but look away when they become bored, hesitant, or non-fluent. (2) *Channel Control.* Eye contact occurs to signal that the communication channel is open and either establishes an obligation to interact or to disavow social contact by diminishing the gaze. (3) *Nature of the Relationship.* Gaze signals a need for affiliation, involvement, or inclusion, like/dislike, embarrassment, humility, submissiveness, or status. These roles often work in reverse for Indian patients as this Indian patient illustrates:

> *We don't at each other. I have a terrible time with that, because they [clinicians] think if you don't look right in their eyes and talk, like you're ashamed of yourself or what, but it's just not done here.* —Karen (Indian patient)

Eye contact is also used to produce anxiety in others and a gaze of longer than ten seconds is likely to induce discomfort. Gaze is also a high predictive indicator of aggressiveness. Indian patients are especially attuned to prolonged eye contact as uncomfortable. As children, they are taught to turn their eyes away out of respect. This Indian patient adds how the element of kinship is related to eye behavior:

> *Usually we don't do that, straight eye contact, because of the respect. It's just respect, it's not questioning the authority or, um, challenging, so we just focus on a different part of the body or just look down and you may see us look at your eyes, but then we're always focused somewhere else (laugh). Or it may seem that we're looking at you, but we're looking beyond you or at something else. We're not challenging what you're saying. We're listening to what you're saying, trying to learn and understand what you're saying,*

so we're not trying to do the eye contact as a challenge, but as respect. It's a learned behavior, too (laugh). Especially men. —Vine (Indian patient)

It has been argued that what individuals think of as the niceties of social conduct are in fact rules for guiding them in their attachment to and detachment from social gatherings; the niceties themselves providing them the idiom for manifesting this (Goffman, 1963, pp. 247-248). Through linguistic habitus, speakers often follow these rules with very little conscious thought, paying what they feel is but a small tribute to convention. But there are national and ethnic differences that contribute to awkwardness, and there are more extreme eye contact systems.

For example, some tribal cultures forbid the son-in-law to look directly at the mother-in-law. In some tribes, inferiors do not look at superiors. Members of some tribes do not look at each other at all when they are speaking (Klopf, 1991, p. 190). This goes against the cultural training of biomedicine, thus clinicians experience the difference as deviant rather than "different." This Indian patient alludes to the interplay of verbal and nonverbal cues and whether they function to relay personal health information.

It depends on who you're talking to. Like if it was your clan uncle or something like that, or your brother, you wouldn't be gazing into their eyes with direct confrontation. At least that was how I was taught. Sometimes I think they do it out of respect for who you are, and for someone like me they would consider me old even though I don't feel old! I think they'd feel like I was an older person and would respect that. You can tell sometimes in the tone of their [clinicians] voice or how they're speaking with you and their faith in how you're guiding them through this whole process, because it's not easy to walk into these types of places to spill some of your utmost issues out to somebody. —Wendy (Indian patient)

Because of kinship connections and poor health, Indian patients are more apt to refrain from direct eye contact with clinicians who are in a position of authority or are the opposite sex. This does not imply evasion, however, as this Indian patient points out when considering how new clinicians react to Indian eye behavior:

> *I would presume [doctors] are figuring either this person doesn't trust me or doesn't think I'm a good doctor or doesn't really want to be here, and that really isn't the case. People go there [to clinics/hospitals] because they're hurt, because they're sick and they do want the treatment, but at the same time they're not going to, people don't react the same way. And again, you'd be surprised, and again back to the modesty. We [in-laws] probably wouldn't even be in the same location together without somebody else being there at the same time. So it goes back a long time. The not looking at people, the lack of eye contact has nothing to do with somebody telling you a story or not telling you a story. It's just the way it is.* —David (Indian patient)

When individuals of any culture are in the presence of others, they respond to communicative events. Their gazes, looks, and postural shifts carry a variety of implications and meanings. Adults are accomplished in producing all of these effects and are adeptly perceptive in catching their significance when performed by accessible others. This is inherent in the Indian linguistic habitus that is quite the opposite from non-Indian clinicians as this example highlights:

> *Growing up your entire life, you're not to stare [eye contact]. When you turn away from your elder, you kind of turn away just out of respect. It's kind of threatening to keep looking at them in the eyes. I think a lot of elders, even a lot of older people, like my parents age, would feel the same way.* —David (Indian patient)

Everywhere and constantly, eye contact is employed, yet rarely is it systematically examined (Goffman, 1981, p. 1). We become knowing and skilled in regard to the evidential uses made of the appearance of looking. We clear our throat, we pause to think, we turn attention to the next event, and soon we specialize these acts as inherent in habitus, performing them with no felt contrivance. In addition to showing respect, there is a function of showing modesty and not being forward appearing, as explained here:

Eye contact, especially between a man and a woman, where they are not spouse or boyfriend/girlfriend, they're supposed to look away. I don't really look into people's eyes either, especially a man. It's more out of respect and modesty and, among the [tribe/clan], a loose woman is not a good thing. So eye contact could be seen as flirting. —Quail (Indian patient/clinician)

Although the visual channel is used to obtain information conveyed by facial expression and gesture, most of which could be characterized as emotional or affective, the visual channel is also used to convey attention and to determine whether others are paying attention, listening, and following the train of thought. It is not unusual to see Indian speakers sitting or standing side-by-side[67] rather than facing each other when involved in conversation. Western health consultations are usually arranged so that the clinician sits directly facing the patient. This Indian patient describes eye behavior as also alluding to using other nonverbal gestures differently than among non-Indian speakers:

It's not polite to do eye contact. People will talk to you, probably just the way I'm talking to you now, they'll look at you and then look away. It has nothing to do with telling you truths or not truths. It has to do with the culture. Most time, if you hang around the rez long enough, you talk with people, you watch people, they'll stand side-by-side; when in your own culture, you stand eye contact to eye contact, you look eye to eye. People will stand side-by-side and they'll talk to each other and a lot of the elder people they don't even use hand gestures, they won't point. The only thing you'll find is like this, you've probably seen that before with the lips, meaning over there. What do you call that? It's not

---

[67] This was most often the case when taking photographs of friends at their homes and at communal gatherings on reservations.

a sign of weakness. Kind of rude, even if you're pointing at,
if I say this fella, he stays over there where everybody else
does a lot of pointing. Coming out of two cultures we kind
of do both. The doctors will do the head bob to see if they
can keep looking at you. —George (Indian patient)

The visual channel is thus used as well as the auditory channel
to structure attention. This is accomplished in several ways: (1) the
speaker must attract the attention of the listener and convey whose
attention is sought, (2) the prospective listener must recognize that
the speaker is seeking attention, (3) the listener must convey attention to the speaker that the listener is attending, and (4) the speaker
must recognize that the listener is paying attention (Philips, 1983,
pp. 7-8). The social contexts of Indian speakers, however, function
much more subtly and serve to interfere with the clinician's understanding of an Indian patient's attention and interest:

I don't know, Indian people are more passive, they usu-
ally don't look at eye contact to other people, they just kind
of look away. So if you're talking to an older Indian person,
looking at that person in the eye contact is like disrespecting
that person as they're sitting there, I would think. They
would not look at doctors when they're talking [and they see
it] as them not listening to them or them not paying attention
to them. [They should] take it into consideration of your eye
contact, tell that person that you're not disrespecting them
by looking at them in the eye contact. It's not the way they're
used to communicating, and that your type of communica-
tion is what you learned. —Diane (Indian patient)

Because it is common for non-Indians to determine whose attention a speaker is seeking by the alignment and gaze direction of
speakers, who tend to face those they are addressing and to gaze in
their direction to see if they are returning the gaze and paying attention, it is confusing for clinicians to interpret patients who do not
employ this behavior:

A lot of the older people, maybe even the younger ones,
won't look at [clinicians] directly in the eye, but they're still

listening. I think it's from way back, it's kind of like respect.
—Mona (Indian patient)

Non-Indians face more directly and more often when they gaze at others. Indians do not gaze into the faces of those being spoken to as much as non-Indians do and also do not gaze as often at certain individuals more than at others (following Eades, 1994a; Fuller & Toon, 1988; Hall, Roter, et al., 1988; Klopf, 1991; Luckmann, 2000; Philips, 1983). Instead, the speaker's gaze is directed more equally toward those the speaker is facing. This does not mean that Indian speakers never focus their gaze on certain individuals more often than others, but rather that less of their speech is directed this way.[68]

There is some evidence that the gaze direction of the Indian listener in particular is interpreted in a qualitatively different way than non-Indian interactions. The area around the eyes can be, for Indian speakers and hearers, a behaviorally expressive region (Philips, 1983, p. 55). Widening and crinkling the muscles around the eyes modifies speakers' talk. Hearers' attention is to some degree conveyed by changes in facial expressions that involve movement in the areas around the eyes. This would suggest an odd pattern of information exchange in which the most expressive region of the face seems to be the least attended.

Eye contact can have wide cultural variation in the health care setting (Loustaunau & Sobo, 1997, p. 154). The physician's gaze has often been interpreted as vital and therapeutic in that it reflects the knowledge and caring that inspire trust and reassurance. When a patient will not meet the doctor's eyes, on the other hand, it could

---

[68] Eye behavior is addressed as early as infancy. An interesting note is that many Indian babies are put on cradleboards (Philips, 1983, p. 63) for short periods soon after birth. The board can be laid on a piece of furniture or propped up against a wall. Indian infants on cradleboards are taken out in public at earlier ages (within two weeks of birth) and for longer periods than non-Indian babies. There is some evidence that older kinsmen assume a priority of the visual channel over the auditory in the infants' processing of information. Babies on cradleboards are propped up vertically so that they can see what is going on. To facilitate sleep, the board is laid flat and often covered even when the baby is wide awake. In this way, visual stimulation is completely cut off, while auditory stimulation in not, suggesting an orientation to the visual as the channel more compelling of attention. With the non-Indian middle-class infants, by contrast, greater efforts are made to cut off auditory stimulation to provide a soothing environment.

signal cultural values of shame, prevarication, or anger (Shorter, 1985). Philips (1983, pp. 75-77) suggests that doctor-patient roles differ based on differences in age, social class, and occupation in other contexts, as this non-Indian clinician confirms:

A lot of [Indian patients] don't look you in the eye, they look down or away. They talk to you sort of in the corner and tell you about what's going on with them and how they're feeling, what kind of pain they're in or how well they're doing with their disease process, so minimal eye contact [out of] respect is the most likely [reason]. They see the doctor, medicine man, highly revered and won't look upon them. —Evan (non-Indian clinician)

It is usually the person in power who directs and controls the particular pattern of gaze direction and the control of the official structure of talk (ibid.). The clinician also controls or defines the juncture or point at which a shift in addressor-addressee relations occurs. The clinician may cut off a patient's unfinished utterance by beginning to speak, by attending to another, or looking elsewhere, while patients do not typically do this. This Indian elder relays:

I'd get uncomfortable if you kept looking at me long enough, a feeling of disrespect. —Fred (Indian patient)

Ben-Sira (1976; 1980) posits in his social interaction model that because patients come to the medical interaction with anxiety about their medical prognoses, less knowledge about medical techniques than the clinician, and less ability to connect treatments with improvements in health, the affective element of the physician's communication becomes a key aspect of patienta' assessments. The affective factor is the physician's mode of communication, consisting of behavior directed toward the patient as a "person" rather than as a "case" (1980), and is operationalized as the allocation of sufficient time to the interaction, show of interest in the patient, and demonstration of devotion to the medical problem.

Similarly, in a Foucaultian manner, the physician touches the patient to diagnose illnesses. They touch their patients as though they were objects or "nonpersons," thereby preventing feelings about invasion of privacy (Klopf, 1991, p. 1). On the other hand, it is possible for one person to treat others as if they were not there at all and not worthy of close scrutiny (Goffman, 1963, p. 83). Moreover, it is possible for the individuals, by their staring or "not seeing," to alter their own appearance hardly at all in consequence of the presence of the others, as the "nonperson" treatment. Eye behavior has the power to make individuals in a social context visible or invisible, without being aware of that power.

> *A bad attitude is like you don't, like when someone's there and they just happen not to see you, they just ignore you. Like the pharmacy people, they just walk past me and don't even turn. I'm like, hello, I'm right here.* —Gertrude (Indian patient)

In my field notes, not only did I observe, but I also reacted to the actual topic I was evaluating. Because I was cognizant of differences in eye contact, I made sure I respected this aspect of communicating and took particular care to arrange the interviews with eye gaze in mind. Well over half of the Indian individuals I interviewed did not maintain direct eye contact with me for more than short periods of time. I made it a point to position my chair at an almost side-by-side angle that would allow either myself and/or my interview partner to choose whether to look at each other or to look away. For those whom I could tell barely liked any eye contact at all, I found myself shifting my chair even more so in order to sit directly side-by-side. Of those who did not mind eye contact, there was still gaze disconnection at longer intervals than I am used to, but I got used to looking away while talking and listening to their stories. This was easier to do than refraining from interrupting, as I noted:

> •He sat looking straight ahead. We were in a row of chairs in the quiet area of the waiting area. We sat with an empty chair between us, and his son and daughter-in-law sat a few seats away at the end of the row beyond him, not next to him. Because he looked straight ahead at the wall, I did the same. Every now and then I looked over to see where he was looking. Sometimes when I turned toward him, he glanced at me, then turned away again.

•She told me right off she didn't want me looking at her. I moved my chair a bit more away than the side-by-side it already was to remind myself not to face her. This is very different for me, because I am used to reading facial expressions and gestures, along with listening to words. It almost felt like I was keeping my eyes closed. The experience of talking this way made me think of confessional chambers or darkened hospital rooms. Besides being polite, looking away does give people more permission or freedom to say what they are thinking, if no one is reading things into every motion or expression they make. It makes me wonder if eye contact not only can add to communications but also subtract. We finish talking, and I turn off the recorder and ask her to select a gift. She is delighted and looks at me when she thanks me. I thank her as well and look at her briefly.

•I notice that as I have been taking photographs of people, with explicit permission, they are most often seated side-by-side while talking and gazing at a distant point somewhere ahead of them. When people who are kin and speaking personally, the photographs show that they neither face each other nor look directly into the other's eyes.

Eye contact has the power to connect, disrupt, evade, or interrupt conversations, which is critical to health care decisions and affects the comfort levels of both clinician and patient. The culture of biomedicine teaches that good practice means maintaining eye contact and gazing at the patient. Some experienced clinicians do part of their physical examination while taking a patient's history. They observe skin, hair, eyes, breathing, clothes, and smell. When the patients are Indian, however, this biomedical training often can work against building communicative relationships.

Touch and Physical Proximity

Touch and physical distance in communicative encounters are other forms of nonverbal communication. Touch conveys many meanings. It can be used to connect with others and establish feelings of warmth, approval, emotional support, and intimacy. On the other hand, touch can communicate anger, aggression, frustration, and a desire to control others by invading their personal space. Touch (or a laying on of hands) may also be regarded as therapeutic. Cultures have specific guidelines for times and situations when it is acceptable to touch others (Luckmann, 2000, p. 55). Middle-class mainstream Americans typically consummate a business deal with a handshake; some Indians, however, view a firm handshake as aggressive and even offensive. Additionally:

> *Yeah, you kind of jump back a little bit [for blood pressure or vital signs] because that's just the way you're kind of taught. I think for initial appointments, a handshake's good enough.* —Vine (Indian patient)

The use of touch is subject to strict (although varying) cultural rules, depending on the situation and on the age, gender, and relationship of the parties. A non-Indian clinician may choose to shake hands with a new patient (or one not seen for some time), but it would not be surprising if this ritual were to be omitted with new Indian patients. In Western cultures, doctors often express sympathy for a distressed patient by touching an arm or hand (Katz, 1984, p. 51). With Indian patients, however, rules may delineate when men may touch women, affected by factors such as whether the woman is menstruating, as well as kinship relations. A doctor's reassuring touch may hence be experienced as distressing or even as a sexual advance.

Avoidance of touch, on the other hand, can convey derision, disrespect, and refusal. Patterns of touch vary widely from culture to culture, though. What one culture permits, another may not. Edward T. Hall (1969, pp. 13, 57-58) theorizes that, with regard to touch, two general classes exist among cultures of the world. Contact cultures allow much contact, and non-contact cultures permit little contact between culture members. People in contact cultures communicate in closer proximity to each other. They touch more, face one another more directly, and utilize more eye contact than those in non-contact cultures. In addition to kinship rules, Indian patients prefer much less contact and request to have clinicians ask for permission before touching them. Touch is not just a form of assurance:

[T]here's a long line of custom about touching. For in-stance, the son-in-law never talks to his mother-in-law or touches her, ever. They go through their whole lives that way . . . and when a doctor or a nurse or somebody touches an elder, they're insulting them. —Jackie (Indian patient/clini-cian)

Back to the same thing, asking people about [touching] instead of telling them: being aware that it's a different way, people are different. Maybe they really are. People here are really different than the outside in the sense that, I keep going back to the modesty issue—asking, "Can I touch you?" There's some people that, there's huggers and there's non-huggers. Being more sensitive to the fact. See, a lot of Indian people can be in severe pain and they won't say anything. So it's a little bit more difficult for [clinicians] to elicit. They have to learn a different way to elicit infor-mation from the patient than they are used to. The biggest part, male and females, especially the older ones, it's be-cause it's a warrior culture and when you're hurt, you don't say anything. You suck it up. They have a term around here they call it "cowboy it up." —David (Indian patient)

Touch-avoidant people, like in many Indian cultures, feel un-comfortable in situations requiring touch, and they have negative feelings toward touching and being touched. High touch avoiders feel tension, dislike, and resentment when they are touched and are unlikely to reciprocate. They remain aloof, especially avoiding touching the opposite sex. In the clinic setting, this is disconcerting to clinicians who expect to touch their patients during examinations. Many patients avoid seeking health care precisely for this reason:

I think they try. It's just a personal thing. Some people can be touched or whatever, and others, they don't go [to the clinic] unless they have to because that [touching] is a problem. That's just not part of, there is a definite separa-tion of the sexes in these cultures. —Emilie (Indian patient)

I personally don't touch, because I don't need to, and I've learned not to. The only time is if I have worked with someone for a long time and perhaps, you know, on the hand or something like that, and never, and it would be only with a female or a child. That is different than other places.
—Paula (non-Indian clinician)

Being touched requires a sense of comfort and familiarity with a clinician. With the prevailing practices of contract care and "rent-a-docs," it is often difficult to maintain a sense of continuity of relationship which, in turn, interferes with conducting what may seem like routine examination procedures. This Indian patient illustrates the widespread dislike of being touched:

Again I think that all goes back to, it might be an issue in the beginning when you've got a new doctor coming in, but when people began to see that doctor a lot more, when they see their faces on a weekly or, for some people, a daily basis, I think they begin to feel more comfortable with that person. Even then you don't know the doctor as well as you would know your aunt or your uncle or your mother or dad. Yes, I think most people probably do get uncomfortable with anybody touching them that they don't know too well. It seems that they're a little more comfortable with the doctors that are there and have been there for years. —David (Indian patient)

There is also not usually any mechanism in place in Indian health systems that allows for maintaining such belief practices and behavioral preferences. When such occasions occur, confusion, dissatisfaction, and annoyance can add to problems in meeting the health needs of the patient. This non-Indian clinician explains a situation where an Indian father prohibited White clinicians from touching his very sick child because of "evil qualities" he attributed to race:

The one [instance] I know for sure, it's because I was White, because they stated so and that I was possessed by the devil, they said. And so you know, you just kind of talk your way through that because there was nobody that was

Native here at that time, because it was a weekend at the ER, and there was nobody here that I could have do vitals on this baby that needed vitals, so I just explained. You have to almost agree and be on their side against yourself, because your priority is that baby. I don't care how he feels about me. I just want to get that baby taken care of.

There was another nurse at the time and she didn't handle it as well, and I understand that. It was tough because [the father] was telling us that we were awful people and that we were White. He didn't want our evilness to attach to the baby, so the baby was very sick you could tell by looking. And so I understood that and I would ask his permission to do every single thing, and that worked well. Is it okay if I do this? I'm going to find out how her oxygen's doing right now, because we want to find out, so when we call the doctor at [the hospital] we can tell him where she's leveling at. And just explain every step and trying not to touch as much as possible but giving as much information on vitals as you can. Having him help you out so that you didn't touch the baby. But the other nurse didn't handle it as well, I asked her to step away.

She just told him that the baby is sick, we need to do this, and that wasn't going to work. She didn't have the mental capacity to be able to deal with that. All I cared about was getting this baby's vitals and getting this baby out of here so they can make it to [the hospital], that's all I cared, so that they can get the baby there and they can address her issues.

He wanted to take the baby, because there was going to be a White man in the ambulance, and he was actually the EMT clinician and the other person was the driver and she was Native and so they had to switch, and [the father] had to have it verified and documented and witnessed that he refused because he couldn't go with the ambulance for some reason. But the EMT could not touch that baby on the way there, so anyway the baby did make it to [the hospital] safely, which is great. But anyway, the Native, instead of driving, was a passenger, so that she could be with the baby in the car seat and just monitor and hopefully get there. It was her respirations and her respiratory system that was *failing. That's the best we had. At least we got her to [the hospital].*

[The White EMT] could probably coach her as far as if she needed [to be] intubated on the way there. He was not allowed to do it because of the father. We really didn't have anything in place for that. There's only been rare occasions of that. Usually people want their sick baby, wherever, they'll get well, whatever you gotta do. —Lynn (non-Indian clinician)

In addition to touch and its implications, many Indian patients are also more sensitive to the private space surrounding them in speaking encounters. How human beings use space to communicate is called proxemics, a term Edward T. Hall (1969, p. 1) coined to suggest proximity, the state of being near. The way people use space is determined by their age, gender, status, and cultural orientation. The use of space differs across cultures. The distance kept in social interactions affects the impressions others develop and affects their ease in communicating (Klopf, 1991, p. 197). More distance is required when being with a stranger for this Indian patient:

I believe there would have to be three or four feet of distance, especially if it's a stranger. I know I wouldn't want somebody coming in my space if I didn't know them.
—Wendy (Indian patient)

Distance also determines how eye contact, touch, and vocal volume are used, and provides information about the relationships between people. Standing too far away may appear unfriendly, cold, or perhaps anxious in non-Indian contexts, whereas being too close may feel uncomfortable and appear pushy or insensitive to Indians.

Groups are clearly distinguishable from each other in some contexts (for the most part in private life), and indistinguishable in others (predominantly in public life), or where content is quite similar but structure varies (Hall, 1969, p. 182). Proxemic patterns are only a few of the many differences that enable people to distinguish one group from another. Indian patients experience standing too closely as aggressive and tend to move back in order to increase the social distance:

[It is best] to listen and not be as . . . someone that's as-
sertive can be seen as being aggressive and pushy or some-
thing like that. If you just walk up to an older man or an
older woman that's an Indian or even a younger person, and
you're standing there talking to them and you stand too
close to them or you're talking loudly to them, they see that,
too, as being aggressive. They don't see it as what your
opinion is when you're talking to them; they see it as I want
to get away from this person because this person is too
pushy. So when you go to the clinic up here, and I talk to
the doctor, the doctor is talking really fast and really loud
and has to get out of the room and go on to the next patient.
Whereas the nurse, I had one that was a Native American
and the other one was a non-Indian. The Native American
nurse was really nice, she did my blood pressure and every-
thing and she visited for a minute. That's comfortable. The
non-Indian nurse came in and she visited with me for a mi-
nute, because I think she's been there for a while, so she
knows the people. So I think that's why she was more com-
fortable. —Charlotte (Indian patient)

Overcrowding and density can have a profoundly negative effect
on communicative behavior (Knapp, 1972, pp. 41-42). In different
situations, when discussing divergent topics, "comfortable" distances vary. Sometimes participants move closer or back up when
speaking to find a comfortable conversational distance. Distances
that are too close for a given interpersonal situation can elicit negative attitudes when the communicator-addressee relationship is not
an intimate one. Clinicians who are dominant speakers tend to
choose specific seats that will vary depending on the office setting,
the task and the nature of the relationship of the speakers. Spatial
behavior, like communication behavior should be treated as a function of the behavior of the parties communicating. Indian patients in
IHS clinics clearly experience close proximity as negative and inva-
sive:

I think the distance thing [is a problem]. I don't want
somebody in my face and just getting too close physically.
That's very irritating. Four or five feet apart is okay. And

then the demeanor. I'm just thinking of a couple that came to my house and I had a bad foot and couldn't get off the couch. They just kind of invaded my space, I didn't invite them, they were non-Indian and they just came and sat on my coffee table, too. And you don't sit on a coffee table. And then they just got on my face and stared at me and I had no way of getting off the couch and I didn't want to hurt their feelings.

A lot of times I think you have to be invited. But then again I was a [professional], I know how it is to drop by or that you have to see those people. And a lot of times it'll be a short visit. And then if they're busy, I'll say, well, I'll be back. A lot of times I don't go into the house if they don't want me to, but at least you can learn a lot even from the yard, and eventually they will let you in or they won't let you in. And especially like if a young mother is bathing her baby and there I am, inconsiderate and trying to do my whole visit while she's busy. Or if there's a lot of family people visiting then I'll say, well I'll be back. And it may take a few visits. It's not going to happen right away, but eventually we become friends. I think in the end we develop a friendship.

The example came [with me]; it's a natural example of my experience as a young mother. [Visitors] did come in, somebody did, inconsiderate, they just kind of were not sensitive. I think it's a personal thing. If you're a courteous, considerate person, I think you would do well [on the reservation]. I would say respect is a very big issue for native people. —Emilie (Indian patient)

Being aware and respectful of Indian patients' personal space and sense of privacy are critical factors clinicians need to respond to in order to keep their patients coming in to the clinic and to provide better care. By invading personal space, their patients may withdraw not only physically but conversationally as well.

The following comments are from the field notes I made both during and after the interviews about touch and proximity:

•I have learned from some of my close Indian friends that they do not want and will not allow themselves to be touched, even for a greeting, parting hug, or arm around the shoulder. Therefore, I was very careful not to touch anyone I interviewed, whether Indian or not, so as to avoid interfering with my own interview process. If someone wanted to shake my hand or touch my arm, I would reciprocate in a parallel manner if I thought it was welcomed, or if I felt like it myself.

•When I set up my chair to speak with people, not only did I turn my chair at a direction to avoid direct eye gaze, but I also set it at what I thought was a comfortable distance, slightly more than I am used to. I allowed the person I was talking with to make any change in chair arrangement. None of the people moved their chairs to be either farther or closer. The distance was about three to four feet apart.

•I experienced great warmth from a few of the females I interviewed and felt as though I wanted to give them a hug by the time we finished our interview. Unlike my usual behavior, I waited to see if they initiated any form of touch and only one female did. One male who is the husband of one of my close Indian friends gave me a hug when I parted, but he had gone to the university and has worked off the reservation as a professional for many years.

•I have known a woman at Fort Belknap for years and we feel like we are family—a very close relationship, like an aunt. Even though I am always so happy to see her each visit, she told me from our first meeting not to touch or hug her—ever. It goes against my own feelings of warmth and expressiveness to not hug her, so I make the arm motions of a hug from a distance, and that seems to work for us.

Time

Handling of time represents a very common source of nonverbal misunderstanding (Hall, 1969, p. 182) and critically affects the process of health care. A significant dimension of culture is that each culture has its own concept of time (Klopf, 1991, p. 198). Cultures take their own time system for granted and believe others operate within the same time frame.[69] Time is money to White Americans and they realize that only so much is available in life. Thus they want to use it wisely. Promptness is essential, and people who are late have often been experienced as having committed an offense.

> *I don't know how much training doctors have in commu-*
> *nication. And they like to get to the point because they don't*
> *have a lot of time but that's not necessarily a Native way.*
> —Emilie (Indian patient)

> *And because of the way IHS is set up, say you go to a*
> *private physician, and if you don't keep your appointment*
> *when it's supposed to be, they're not too happy with that,*
> *because you know that's money to them. It is here (IHS), too,*
> *but because they can come in freely and leave, you know it's*
> *kind of harder to deal with.* —Mona (Indian patient)

It is conventional in Western mainstream cultures to be on time, or a few minutes early for appointments such as seeing a doctor, but it is customary to be a few minutes late for social engagements in someone's home (Fuller & Toon, 1988, p. 29). Indian cultures take time commitments more lightly; people are frequently late. Western cultures think of time in linear-spatial terms, specifically past, present, and future time and something to be manipulated, made up, saved, spent, and wasted. Time is an aspect of history rather than a part of an immediate experience. The present is a steppingstone between the past and future. Activities are not interrupted in order to "be on time." When the event is over, then people will head to the appointment.

There has been a failure to accept the reality of different cultures within American national boundaries. Indians are treated as though they are recalcitrant and undereducated. Middle-class Americans of northern European heritage live in culturally differentiated enclaves with their own communication systems, institutions, and values.

---

[69] Edward Hall (1990, pp. 173-174) divides principle differences in how cultures handle time into monochromic and polychromic cultures. In *monochromic* cultures, Western people do things in order, following schedules, where time can be wasted, squandered, or saved. In *polychromic* cultures, such as Indian cultures, people do many things at once, and relationships come before schedules.

Much richness is missed by not addressing difficulties and differences, leading often to unexpected consequences.

It would be useful for the non-Indian to be able to recognize the culturally relevant signals indicating when something has begun, is continuing, or has ended. Two aspects of participant regulation that are cues include the frequency of activities in which only one person is necessary to begin an activity, with others joining in as they arrive; and the frequency of movement in and out of activities by people, as the activities themselves continue. The notion of "Indian time" is widespread among North American Indians. It usually seems to have a boundary-maintenance function in that it is always something viewed as peculiarly Indian.

Methods different cultural groups use to value time can create challenges in the health care system. For example, clinicians who work in the operating room must be both future- and present-oriented (Luckmann, 2000, pp. 266-267). To plan and adhere to an operating room schedule, the person must be future-oriented and abide by the calendar and clock. However, once the surgical procedure commences, the surgeon and other health care professionals must switch to the present orientation (Giger & Davidhizar, 1999). This Indian patient explains her frustration with experiences of IHS medical time:

> *But you kind of know, it's kind of known in the community that if you have an emergency, you go to [one of the facilities]. They're slow. Their emergency room, like, they're not that busy. I don't know. One of my friends had to go into the emergency that one time, and I took her over there and she, like she was sick, and they made her stand out in the waiting room. They didn't even give her a chair or anything, and we stood out there for like, I don't know, about 45 minutes, and she didn't get to see a doctor, and she was like jerking. She was, man, you could die waiting to get into the emergency room, but it's the truth, I mean, and like my dad.*
>
> *Oh, this is another story, like my dad, we live out in the country and he hemorrhaged and he had like internal bleeding, and they called the ambulance, and the ambulance didn't show up for a hour and a half! Like by the time he got into the doctor, like he was almost ready to die. They thought he*

was almost ready to die 'cause he had bled so much, like an hour and a half to get the ambulance there! [The health facility] is about 15 minutes away. I think they said they have only two ambulances for our whole reservation. One was up in [the city] already on a call and another one was like handling another call all the way across the reservation. So that just goes back to the money issue. And my dad was just in line waiting for a ambulance, I guess. But they were like really surprised when they got him in, and they ended up flying him out to [the city]. He just went right into surgery, because he was like in such bad shape. He just like he said he felt sick all day, and he was like on this blood thinner medicine, and he had just had surgery, and he said he felt sick, and then pretty soon he started getting light-headed, and then he just started going out of consciousness, and he had a feeling it might be that blood thinner. It turns out his stitches opened inside and there was no way, if he was on blood thinner, there was no way to stop his bleeding, but they said he lost, I can't remember how much, but like a big percentage of the blood in his body he lost. He was lucky he made it. —Carla (Indian patient)

Furthermore, appointment systems are designed to assume that patients will visit the doctor one at a time, and it is important that one patient has one appointment, if it is desired to keep on time (Fuller & Toon, 1988, p. 29):

[I]t's so hard to get in there. Like to get an appointment, it's a lot of trouble . . . they just have a lot of people to serve. Like, you can to go to the walk-in clinic, but you have to be there like 8:00 in the morning to sign in, and sometimes you're not the first person there, so like every time I go to the walk-in clinic, I spend most of the day there just waiting to see the doctor, and it's a lot better if you can go someplace else and just make an appointment. If you make an appointment, you have to be thinking ahead, because it has, like where I go to [on the reservation], like if you want your woman's exam, you have to make that about three months in advance, because they're at that clinic only certain

amounts of the day. Same thing, if it's like your eyes or to see the dentist, you have to think ahead and make your appointment. And when you're a student, that's kind of a pain, because you're only gonna be home for like a week at a time or something. —Carla (Indian patient)

The problem of time is always very crucial in health care. Usually, it takes more time than the physician has available to address the patient's concerns. However, the quantity of time available is not as important as the quality and intensity of the relationship, and the clinician's concentration (Luban-Plozza, 1995). Even if expectations are not expressed openly, patients may have an "unformulated latent need" for information and support (Pratt, Seligmann, et al., 1957). This, however, is not necessarily consciously accessible, connected to the immediate event, experienced as an acceptable thought, or presented to clinicians if they do not ask about it (Blatterbauer, Kupst, et al., 1976). Given the realities of the present system, clinicians have neither the time nor the opportunity to meet all of a patient's expectations, especially the latent ones.

They don't have enough time to see every patient. These doctors can't do everything they should for all these patients, because they've got too many. —Alan (Indian patient)

The nurses seem to be okay, but it seems like the doctors are always in a hurry, because the last time I went there, she was like really fast and then she was gone. But once they finish that examination, it seems like they're in a rush to get going. Being talked to really fast because they're trying to get out the door. I always show up to my appointments on time. —Diane (Indian patient)

It was difficult to experience the differences in perceptions of time. I have been brought up with an excessively strong sense of linear time, being on time, being afraid of being late, and even having nightmares about showing up late for important events such as final exams. I represent almost the opposite sense of time than most Indians, especially if it has to do with a scheduled appointment or event. Interestingly, however, during my personal unplanned time,

I behave very similarly to "Indian time" and prefer the open-endedness of "going with the flow." The following anecdotes are from my field notes:

•I showed up for my prearranged appointment with the IHS Unit Director right on time. I went to the receptionist and let her know I was here for my appointment. She said, "Oh, he's not here today. He's in [the city] all day." I was really surprised because I planned my whole trip around this appointment. Right at the moment I realized this, I understood my habitus was at work. Surely he would have let me know, I thought. Wrong. Either he's here or he's not here. Now it's up to me to just keep going on with my plans for the day. The receptionist tells me she sees me in his appointment schedule and offers to arrange for me to speak with someone else. I am impressed that she takes the initiative to make a substitution, and she shows me waiting areas where I can talk to patients in the meantime. Though not apologetic, she certainly makes sure I am welcome. Obviously, I am thankful.

•At the appointed time (of course), I show up to meet with the doctor. I am shown into his office and given a seat. After about 20 minutes, he pokes his head in and says he's running late and asks if I mind waiting for him. He shows me some books I can look at, and so I do. I also begin to write notes about time while I am waiting. He comes in and gives me his full attention, until he is called out to finish an exam consultation. He tells me he will be back. It is almost a half hour before he returns. I occupy myself with his books and writing notes, but keep thinking that I'm "wasting time," when I could be interviewing other people. Not that it is a waste waiting for him, but I am feeling impatient that my "agenda" is not keeping its pace. I am thinking about "Indian time" and also that there seems to be a parallel practice of "doctor time." This amuses me and I decide to keep track if there are parallels between the two. I finish my interview and am glad I waited since our conversation is very interesting, and he has a unique point of view that I feel privileged to hear. When I leave, the facility is about to close and, though I quickly think I didn't get much done, I realize I've learned a lot about time while asking other people about the concept of time.

•As I sit here talking to a woman in the waiting room, I realize I have a set appointment in five minutes. It is in the same building, so I won't have far to go. Our conversation continues past the appointment time and I have simultaneous thoughts: I am (anxiously) aware that I am already late for the appointment; I am interested in continuing the conversation; and I figure if everyone else runs on "Indian time," why can't I? After I have the last thought, I relax and decide to switch to Indian time for the rest of my interviews. This is a great relief to me, and I feel my body relax as well.

•She seems glad to have something to do while she is waiting for her appointment. Her two children (about four and six years old) are playing, walking around, and watching the television that is mounted high up on the wall. The waiting room is not very quiet because it seems to be a hub where people meet with each other, catch up on family news, and exchange stories and laughter. The children move freely in and out of the interview space but do not interrupt us. If anything, it is me who draws my attention to the children and I engage with them. I give them magic markers, a "shorty" pen, and a flashlight that I've brought for children. They are very pleased and spend the rest of our interview time using them. During the interview, she will stop talking to me and talk to someone she knows for five minutes or so. I turn off the recorder while she visits. There is no disruption or apology, but this kind of visiting is normal, even during "an interview." I am able to hear what they talk about and it's about the goings on with their families and an upcoming event they are looking forward to. We continue our conversation until she is called in for her appointment that is about an hour later than her scheduled time.

•I am aware that the demographics and social structure of the reservation are inherent aspects of Indian time. If family is visiting, then the appointment waits. If the person driving to the facility is with family or friends, then the ride to the appointment will be delayed. Kinship plays an important role in how time is used or divided. Once inside a facility, there are differences in time perception between patients and clinicians. The temporal structures we live by are so embedded that it is very difficult to switch to another cultural system of dealing with time.

Time can be experienced as either fluid of fixed, depending on one's place in cultural positioning. But the experience of being trained in a certain regard to time makes it difficult to adjust or change one's position. What seems normal to one culture is strange and uncomfortable to another. Navigating a different habitus of time can be flawed and unsuccessful because of the lack of cultural meaning and positioning.

6
RESEARCH IMPLICATIONS

Theories of cross-cultural sociolinguistics, habitus, Western bio-medicine, and health beliefs are the interconnected foundations upon which sociolinguistic differences in the use of everyday English among Indians and non-Indians in the material health care settings on Montana reservations can be investigated. There is no such thing as a "common use of everyday English" when talking about Indian health care.

If Indian patients spoke only Crow or Assiniboine, and their clinicians only English, it would be evident to everyone that their language differences would require translators and dual language dictionaries or applications to even begin to create mutual understandings between them. The results of this inquiry indicate that it is not only the use of "different" languages that cause miscommunications, but that the English that is "seemingly shared" is based on entirely different linguistic meanings, assumptions, and interpretations.

It might be commonly thought that differing systems of cultural beliefs about disease and healing would be the central challenge in reservation health care. However, the Indians and clinicians (Indian and non-Indian) in this inquiry do not experience these as the main problem. Those who believe in traditional ways often see no conflict with Western medicine and continue to use a combination of traditional healing and biomedicine. When they do make the decision to utilize reservation medical facilities, what they are hoping for and expecting to receive are the optimal benefits that biomedicine has to offer. Their frustrations, therefore, are not primarily caused by different conceptions of disease or healing but with the process of communication that occurs when they seek health care.

The results of this investigation and from the individual's narratives indicate that both Indians and clinicians experience the miscommunications between them as the major factor that interferes with optimal health care at the exact point where verbal and nonverbal language encounters are embodied as emanations of habitus. People live, breathe, and create language in their daily activities with no awareness of their cultural preferences or differences, where the same speech acts are used in different ways and with different cultural meanings. Though clinicians and Indian patients may think they share a language code, they mostly do not. Precisely because differences in worldview and culture are embedded in actions, and since speech is one of the most central actions of cultural habitus and language, complicated differences in linguistic use cause problems where often nothing either speaker is saying is in concordance with the other.

Specific areas of linguistic differences identified in these narratives indicate that disparities in the use of narratives and/or questions, gratuitous concurrence, politeness, respect, silence, gossip, gender, trust, eye contact, touch, proximity, and time are not small details but, in fact, have dramatic effects. A gap exists as wide as if two different languages were being spoken, but almost no one is aware of the profundity of it.

Clinicians and patients alike must learn about these gaps in their linguistic differences if they hope to be able to effectively communicate, which is required for delivering and receiving the best possible health care. Everyone must be able to develop linguistic competency, levels of comprehension, and procedures to collaborate and be knowledgeable in the endeavor of health care. Critical issues of individual miscoding of sociolinguistic behaviors cause speakers to not know what others are talking about when speech becomes desequenced, since so much of clinical practice depends on the patient as a verbal informant. It is in everyone's best interest to develop means of providing information to all involved in the health care process to at least be cognizant about the differences in language production and reception in order to participate more fully in a shared communicative dialogue.

While there have been tremendous gains in the use of technology, medicine does not rely solely on biomedical technology. Medicine at its best is based on language and communication. A medical experience begins with a patient's chief complaint that is the quintessential enactment of language and habitus, and where the verbal description of illness is the starting point of an interaction. The clinician needs to be able to interpret what the patient means and be able to move beyond culture and personality in order to navigate successfully through the diagnostic procedure and treatment.

Clinicians shift from an initial chief complaint to a differential diagnosis based on the verbal and nonverbal language competencies they exchange with their patients. Without intertwined competencies, the likelihood of arriving at the correct diagnosis or treatment is surely hindered. All phases of the medical encounter require communication. Even the "technological" part of medicine requires clear communications. A procedure as simple as obtaining a blood cholesterol level necessitates an understanding of "fasting," a urine specimen entails understanding what a "clean catch" is, and surgical procedures involve "informed consent."

The complicated management of chronic illnesses requires ongoing complexities of interactive management strategies that include addressing behavioral modifications and medication regimens. Even in situations where differences of habitus, power, and linguistic competencies are not as discrepant as they are between Indians and non-Indians, chronic care still presents an enormous challenge to clinician-patient communicative abilities. The fact that lack of compliance is a repeated observation of clinical studies underscores this fact.

When clinicians progress through the diagnostic and treatment phase of medicine, there are myriad junctures where communications can go wrong and lead to the setting up of entire chains of events that result in incorrect courses of action. Much of medicine always did and always will depend on the communicative "relationship" between the clinician and the patient. Again, research shows that this is not referencing a minor issue of politeness or small talk. Miscommunication is a process that can ultimately mean the difference between life and death. Making this communicative leap is not as simple as knowing whether to touch or not. What is required is the ability to develop as much mutual understanding as possible and to understand the parameters that produce successful communications. It is also critical to allow sick patients to seek help and to encourage the clinicians who are willing to help them.

In biomedicine, co-production and collaboration for diagnosis, treatment, and compliance are required for successful health care. Clinicians and patients need to become aware of their own linguistic habitus and learn to talk, listen, connect, and track each other in a sophisticated manner in order to make improvements in the communicative progress. Clinicians need to communicate with their patients with an awareness of how Indians understand the world and use different codes of English; and Indians need to understand the language and assumptions of biomedicine in order to provide necessary information. Competency needs to be developed to reduce the effects of "two different English languages."

A beginning step toward remedying this serious situation requires isolating the productive and receptive linguistic differences and the assumptions that accompany them in order to realize the catastrophic effects they have on Indian morbidity and mortality when clinicians are unaware of enormous linguistic differences. A summary of findings from this investigation of cross-cultural linguistic assumptions and beliefs lays out groundwork for the delineation of potential assumptive barriers.

Future researchers, sociolinguists, and practitioners can utilize this information to further explore the nature of particular cultural and communicative difficulties and to design training programs. Each of the elements is significant and must be brought to light. Both Indians and non-Indians can be trained to recognize differences, after which awareness needs to be converted into continued praxis and eventually to change. At this point, the chasm has the potential to be bridged, if not in daily practice but in awareness and recognition.

Values, Attitudes, Behaviors, and Perceptions

Values	Indian Attitudes & Behaviors	Non-Indian Perceptions
Language	Many cultural elements are contained within the context and meaning of Indian usage of the English language. Differences reflect habitus and worldview and are not easily recognized as being different than Standard English and the corresponding assumptions of meanings. Traditional aspects of Indian culture are	Assumptions are based on Standard English and the Western mainstream habitus. Differences in Indian English are experienced as deviant and insufficient. There is no concept for understanding that cultural differences are reflected in spoken, bodily,

	reflected in both spoken and body English.	and written Standard English.
Kinship	All of extended family is referred to in similar terms such as cousin, auntie, grandmother, etc. The role distinctions of extended family in raising children, however, have little distinction, except where kinship taboos exist. Clans and kindship are "family."	Only the immediate family is considered to be relatives who are responsible for children, and if other relatives step in, then the parents must not be performing their responsibilities adequately.
Caution	Caution is used in personal interactions where information and family problems are not freely revealed to others, but kept within the family. There is also a hesitancy regarding acceptance from others.	Indians may appear to be aloof and reserved, superficial, and thus untrustworthy to non-Indians.
Modesty	Even when people do well and achieve something, they should remain modest. It is embarrassing to remain undressed in the doctor's office or to be touched, looked in the eye, or interrupted.	Indians may not speak of their accomplishments and are usually unconcerned with special achievements. They seem aloof and back away from being too close or touching.
Time	Time is generally flexible and geared to the current activity. It is focused on personal interactions and family. Events happen when a gathering begins to occur.	A different attitude about time is often interpreted as irresponsible and uncaring. It is difficult to know when Indian events start or stop.

Orientation to the Present	There is a quality of being in the present, which is linked to the idea that one should be more interested in being than in becoming. Connections are not experienced as sequential or having cause and effect. There is no hurry to reach a goal in the future. Family and friends come before other commitments. Present time is fluid with history and the future.	When Indians are pressured to give up current needs for vague rewards in the future, frustration often is the result. The Western principle of linear time and is confusing when grappling with present-time behaviors.
Health	The individual must be treated in a holistic manner that includes (more than merely the physical plane of health or illness) the human, natural, and spiritual realms. There are traditional forms of healing that address all levels of illness. Some patients request healers or smudging in hospitals.	Being treated by the biomedical model is preferable. Healers and smudging may be allowed at some facilities, but is often misunderstood in its role of healing.
Family	The value and importance of large extended family kinship and clans cannot be underestimated in the support and security they provide. It is common for large families to live in close proximity to one another. Tribal and clan kinship relations are most important. All relatives engage in raising children.	There is often a failure to understand the validity of relatives who function exactly as natural parents do. Many consider the natural parent to be lax in their duties if other family members step in.

Child Rearing	Children are usually with relatives in all situations and learn to be seen and not heard when adults are present. Child rearing tends to be permissive and self-explanatory rather than restrictive. Respect is a crucial behavior.	Parents can be seen as irresponsible for leaving their children with "others," while, in fact they are family kin who share responsibility in child rearing.
Discipline	It is best to avoid demeaning personal criticism and harsh physical discipline and to instead resort to ignoring, frowning, shaming, scolding, ridicule, or withholding praise. Sibling and peer pressure are good forms of control, and withdrawal is a form of disapproval.	Discipline by ridicule may lead to fear of criticism for incorrect or inadequate responses that are viewed as rude and disrespectful.
Age	Tribal elders are treated with great respect because they are valued for wisdom and experience. All family members are responsible for training young children. Elders are the leaders of the tribe.	The mainstream influence of youthfulness may contribute to a generation gap, the loss of language and customs. Elders play an important family role of preservation
History	The historical roots of colonial dominance, broken trust ant treaties, disease, displacement, loss of land, and forced assimilation caused today's collective social suffering.	History has nothing to do with a person's illness. Everyone shares the same history. Indian history is subservient to Western history.
Cultural Pluralism	Retaining as much of traditional culture as possible is desired, while resisting the forces of assimilation. Indians prefer to stay among themselves rather	Misunderstandings and confusion result when Indians appear to be assimilated outwardly when

	than going into non-Indian areas or participating in non-Indian activities.	they have not actually accepted non-Indian values.
Cooperation	Cooperation is highly valued and strongly rooted to the past, when cooperation was necessary for survival of the family and tribe. Agreement and cooperation are still important for tribal members.	The competitive spirit of the dominant society is often at odds with this value. If one person states they do not know something, others may make the same claim, even if they have the knowledge.
Autonomy	Value is placed on respect for individual dignity and autonomy, where people are not meant to be controlled.	Non-Indians who attempt to give advice, especially of a personal nature, may be rejected.
Work Ethic	One works to meet immediate personal, family, tribal, or spiritual needs since material accumulation is not valued.	Understanding the value behind work is more important than merely getting things done.
Savings	Seeking to acquire savings accounts and insurance policies for one's own benefit is unlikely to be practiced.	The foregoing of the present use of time and money for future gratification is at odds with this concept.
Generosity	Sharing and generosity are highly valued. Indians freely exchange material goods and food. The most highly respected individuals are those who give most generously.	The desire to share food and hospitality and to make good personal relationships often fails to be recognized or is seen as interruptive to more important events.

Pragmatism	Indians tend to be pragmatic, speaking in terms of the concrete rather than abstractions or theory. Knowledge is holistic and flexible.	When greater emphasis is put on concrete examples, there is less frustration or confusion than with abstract ideas that are often forced into artificial categories.
Spirituality	Indian philosophies tend to be contemplative rather than utilitarian. Religious principles are connected to all aspects of being and integrated into daily life, where human, natural, and spiritual realms are entwined.	When spirituality is disregarded in conversation or practice and a central segment of life is ignored, frustration and disharmony may result.
Group Harmony	Emphasis is placed on the group and the importance in maintaining harmony within the group.	Indians do not forge ahead with individual accomplishments and may not always work well on their own.
Nature	Because traditional life meant living in harmony with nature, respect rather than progress is a priority. The practice of reciprocity acknowledges how one gives back to nature what has been taken. There is gratitude for natural offerings. Land provides but is now owned.	Indians are often repulsed by scientific experiments because of historic assaults. They don't value research based on animal experimentation and see progress as exploitation of nature. Disrespecting land rights by others is fought against as harming nature.

There needs to be a sense of hope and enthusiasm that a communicative bridge can be designed and constructed to bring Indians and their clinicians to a shared understanding of the communications that take place between them. It is commonly understood that clinicians and patients are already overwhelmed, and at present, there is inadequate time or money needed to develop such communicative resources. Both parties must realize that they bear accountability and that the gap cannot be lessened without mutual responsibility, authority, and co-production. However, as future research is conducted in the areas identified in this investigation, all parties will realize how high the stakes are and how much can be gained by focusing on communication strategies.

As with any medical disorder, treatment will not occur until there is movement beyond "distressing symptoms" to a clear "diagnosis" and its treatment. This inquiry is a first step in creating a diagnostic typology to help prevent Indian medical care from being stymied by an unknown communicative "disease."

Long before the causes of infectious diseases were known, there was recognition that a serious problem existed, often called plagues, because large groups of people were dying. Early treatments for such plagues involved quarantines and sanitation, even though the origins and mechanisms were unknown. Eventually the germ theory of disease was developed, recognizing bacteria and viruses as causes of disease. Discovering the source of the problem is critical to the solution. There is quite a difference between Hippocrates's belief that infectious disease was caused by vapors from decaying materials to Pasteur's conclusion that disease was caused by germs.

Just as each germ is specific, isolated, named, and treated, so too must the parallel diseases of miscommunication be isolated, named, and treated. Treatments aimed at specific bacteria were developed with different classes of antibacterials and antibiotics to combat them. A generalized view of improving communication is still too non-specific, just as all infections cannot be cured with a single remedy.

In concordance with their medical education, clinicians are trained to strive to help patients. However, they are taught to work within a communicative paradigm that bears almost no resemblance to that of reservation Indians. For example, the typical categories and questions that clinicians use as they move from a chief complaint to its diagnosis, "what, where, why, how, and to what extent," are a foreign language to many Indians. Indians don't think in these compartmentalized categories, or necessarily in categories at all. The medical communicative system is not prepared to interpret health through narratives or differences in eye contact, silence, or agreements that don't necessarily signify consent. Medicine doesn't yet have mechanisms set up that can process cultural paradigms. Too often, neither clinicians nor Indians realize that they operate under differing communicative paradigms. This realization needs to be more fully integrated into medical training as an attempt to understand how differences in worldviews and linguistic habitus can be catastrophic to Indian health. Likewise, Australian Aborigines are often unjustly sentenced due to miscommunications regarding their rights, comprehension of the laws, and the particulars of the legal system in general as Diana Eades' research confirms. Sociolinguistic research should be another crucial field to dissect when American Indians also face great danger from miscommunications in the legal system where consequences are as dangerous, if not more so, than with poor health care outcomes.

If it were understood how profoundly failures of communication affect Indian health care in the realm of Western biomedicine, surely such major communicative failures would require "a war on miscommunication," worthy of national attention and policy. Let this be the beginning step in recognizing, training, and dealing with a disorder that has long remained undiagnosed. It is critical to understand that not all peoples share the same habitus. Merely acknowledging this fact will not address failures in health care outcomes. Just as clinicians identify diseases as unique causal entities with specific assessments and treatments, more effective and precise definitions of communicative competencies in health care must be discerned, attended to, and tackled in order to bridge the chasms that cause lasting linguistic wounds.

7
REFERENCES CITED

[Hipprocates] (1923). *Hippocrates: On decorum and the physician 2*. (trans. E. H. S. Jones). London: William Heinemann.

Anderson, I. A. (1991). Improving patient and provider communication: A synthesis and review of communication interventions. *Patient Education and Counseling, 17*, 99-134.

Andrulis, D. P. (1998). Access to care is the centerpiece in the elimination of socioeconomic disparities in health. *Annals of Internal Medicine, 129*, 412-416.

Arluke, A., Kennedy, L., & Kessler, R. C. (1979). Reexamining the sick-role concept: An empirical assessment. *Journal Of Health and Human Behavior, 20*, 30-36.

Ashton, C. H., Paterniti, D. A., Collins, T. C., Gordon, H. S., O'Malley, K., Peterson, L. A., et al. (2003). Racial and ethnic disparities in the use of health services: Bias, preferences, or poor communication? *Journal of General Internal Medicine, 18*(2), 146-152.

Australian Law Reform Commission. (1986). Report 31: The recognition of Aboriginal customary laws. Australian government publishing service. Canberra, Australia.

Baer, H., & Singer, M. (1986). Toward a critical medical anthropology. *Social Science & Medicine, 23*, 95-98.

Bain, D. J. G. (1976). Doctor-patient communication in general practice consultations. *Medical Education, 10*(2), 125-131.

Barden, J., Boyer, P., & Red Horse, J. (1993). Ways of knowing: Extending the boundaries of scholarship. *Tribal College, 4*(3), 12-15.

Barry, A. (1993). Constructing a courtroom narrative: A lawyer-witness duet. *Current Issues in Linguistic Theory, 93*, 203-213.

Bartlett, E. E., Grayson, M., Barker, R., Levine, D. M., Golden, A., & Libber, S. (1984). The effects of physician communications skills on patient satisfaction; recall, and adherence. *Journal of Chronic Disease, 37*(9/10), 755-764.

Basso, K. (1970). 'To give up on words': Silence in Western Apache culture. *Southwestern Journal of Anthropology, 26*(3), 213-230.

Basso, K. (2001). *Wisdom sits in places: Landscape and language among the Western Apache*. Albuquerque: University of Nebraska Press.

Battiste, M. (2000). *Reclaiming indigenous voice and vision*. Vancouver: University of California Berkeley Press.

Bauman, R., & Sherzer, J. (1974). *Explorations in the ethnography of speaking* (reissued with a new introduction and bibliography, 1989). Cambridge: Cambridge University Press.

Beck, P., Walters, A. L., & Francisco, N. (1990 [1977]). *The sacred: Ways of knowledge, sources of life*. Tsaile, AZ: Northland.

Becker, G. (1997). *Disputed lives: How people create meaning in a chaotic world*. Berkeley, CA: University of California Press.

Beckman, H. B., & Frankel, R. M. (1984). The effect of physician behavior on the collection of data. *Annals of Internal Medicine, 101*, 692-696.

Ben-Sira, Z. (1976). The function of the professional's affective behavior in client satisfaction: A revised approach to social interaction theory. *Journal Of Health and Social Behavior, 17*, 3-11.

Ben-Sira, Z. (1980). Affective and instrumental components in the physician-patient relationship: An additional dimension of interaction theory. *Journal of Health and Social Behavior, 21*(2), 170-180.

Bernard, H. R. (1994). *Research methods in anthropology: Qualitative and quantitative approaches*. 2nd ed. Walnut Creek, CA: AltaMira Press.

Bernstein, B. (1972). Social class, language and socialization. In P. P. Giglioli (Ed.) *Language and social context*, (pp. 157-178). New York: Penguin.

Berry, J. W., Trimble, J. E., & Olmedo, E. L. (1986). The assessment of acculturation. In W. L. Lonner & J. W. Berry (Eds.), *Field methods in cross-cultural research*, (pp. 291-326). Beverly Hills: Sage Publications.

Billings Area IHS. (n.d.). Retrieved February 21, 2005, from http://www.ihs.gov/FacilitiesServices/AreaOffices/Billings/Bil.asp

Bilmes, J. (1997). Being interrupted. *Language in Society, 26*(4), 507-531.

Bird, M. E. (2002). Health and indigenous people: Recommendations for the next generation. *American Journal of Public Health, 92*(9), 1391-1392.

Blatterbauer, S., Kupst, M. J., & Schulman, J. L. (1976). Enhancing the relationship between physician and patient. *Health and Social Work, 1*(1), 45-57.

Bol, M. C. (1998). *Stars above, earth below: American Indians and nature*. Niwot, CO: Roberts Rinehart.

Bourdieu, P. (1976). The economics of linguistic exchanges. *Social Science Information, 16*(6), 645-668.

Bourdieu, P. (1982b). *Language & symbolic power*. Cambridge, Massachusetts: Harvard University Press.

Bourdieu, P. (1983). The field of cultural production, or the economic world reversed. *Poetics*, *12*(Nov.), 311-356.

Bourdieu, P. (1985). Social space and the genius of groups. *Social Science Information*, *24*(2), 195-220.

Bourdieu, P. (1988). Flaubert's point of view. *Critical Inquiry*, *14*(Spring), 539-562.

Brown, E., & Shaughnessy, T. (Eds.). (1980). *Education for social work practice with American Indian families*. Tempe, AZ: Arizona State University.

Brown, R., & Gilman, A. (1972 [1960]). The pronouns of power and solidarity. In P. P. Giglioli (Ed.) *Language and social context*, (pp. 252-282). New York: Penguin.

Brucker, P. S., & Perry, B. J. (1998). American Indians: Presenting concerns and considerations for family therapists. *The American Journal of Family Therapy*, *26*(4), 307-320.

Bryan, W. L., Jr. (1996). *Montana's Indians: Yesterday and today.* 2nd ed. Helena, MT: American and World Geographic Publishing.

Buller, M. K., & Buller, D. B. (1987). Physicians' communication style and patient satisfaction. *Journal of Health and Social Behavior*, *28*(4), 375-388.

Burke, K. (2000). *On symbols and society*. Chicago: University of Chicago Press.

Calhoun, C., LiPuma, E., & Postone, M. (1993). *Bourdieu: Critical perspectives*. Chicago: Universtiy of Chicago Press.

Canby, W. O. (1998). *American Indian law in a nutshell*. 3rd ed. St. Paul, MN: West Group.

Carillo, J. (1998). *Readings in American Indian law: Recalling the rhythm of survival*. Philadelphia: Temple University Press.

Cegala, D. J., McClure, L., Marinelli, T. M., & Post, D. M. (2000). The effects of communication skills training on patients' participation during medical interviews. *Patient Education and Counseling*, *41*, 209-222.

Charon, R. (2001). Narrative medicine: A model for empathy, reflection, profession, and trust. *Journal of the American Medical Association*, *286*(15), 1897-1902.

Chrisman, N. (1977). The health seeking process. *Culture, Medicine, and Psychiatry*, *1*, 351-378.

Clark, J. A., & Mishler, E. G. (1992). Attending to patients' stories: Reframing the clinical task. *Sociology of Health & Illness*, *14*(3), 344-372.

Coe, R. (1970). *Sociology and medicine*. New York: McGraw-Hill.

Conklin, H. C. (1964). Ethnogenealogical method. In W. H. Goodenough (Ed.) *Explorations in cultural anthropology*, (pp. 22-55). New York: McGraw-Hill.

Cook, M. (1996a). Aboriginal evidence in the cross-cultural courtroom. *Forensic Linguistics*, *3*(2), 273-288.

Cook, M. (1996b). A different story: Narrative versus 'question and answer' in Aboriginal evidence. *Forensic Linguistics*, *3*, 273-288.

Cornell, S. (1988). *The return of the native: American Indian political resurgence*. New York: Oxford University Press.

Daly, M. B., & Hulka, B. S. (1975). Talking with the doctor, 2. *Journal of Communication*, *25*, 148-152.

Davis, M. S. (1968). Variations in patients' compliance with doctors' advice: An empirical analysis of patterns. *American Journal of Public Health*, *58*(2), 274-288.

DeFine, M. S. (1997). A history of governmentally coerced sterilization. Retrieved June 31, 2004, from http://www.geocities.com/9118/mike2.html

Deloria, E. (1998). *Speaking of Indians*. Lincoln, NE: University of Nebraska Press.

Deloria, V., Jr., & Wilkins, D. E. (1992). *Tribes, treaties and constitutional tribulations*. Austin, TX: University of Texas Press.

Deloria, V., Jr., & Wilkins, D. E. (1997). *Red earth, white lies: Native Americans and the myth of scientific fact*. Golden, CO: Fulcrum.

Deloria, V. J. (1991a). American Indian metaphysics. In V. J. Deloria (Ed.) *Indian education in America: 8 essays by Vine Deloria, Jr.* Boulder, CO: American Indian Science and Engineering Society.

Deloria, V. J. (1991b). Commentary: Research, redskins, and reality. *American Indian Quarterly, 15*(4), 457-469.

DeSantis, L. (1994). Making anthropology clinically relevant to nursing care. *Journal of Advanced Nursing, 20*(4), 707-715.

DeVito, J. A. (1998). *The interpersonal communication book*. 8th ed. Boston: Allyn & Bacon.

Di Luzio, A., Günthner, S., & Orletti, F. (Eds.). (2001). *Culture in communication: Analyses of intercultural situations*. Amsterdam: John Benjamins Publishing Company.

Dibben, M. R., Morris, S. E., & Lean, M. E. J. (2000). Situational trust and co-operative partnerships between physicians and their patients: A theoretical explanation transferable from business practice. *Quarterly Journal of Medicine, 93*, 55-61.

Dirven, R., & Putz, M. (1993). State of the art article: Intercultural communication. *Language Teaching, 26*, 144-156.

Doyal, L., & Pennell, I. (1979). *The political economy of health*. Boston: South End Press.

Durkheim, E. (2005 [1938]). What is a social fact? In R. B. McNeal, Jr. & K. Tiemann (Eds.), *Intersections: Readings in Sociology*, (pp. 85-95). Boston: Pearson Custom Publishing.

Eades, D. (1992). *Aboriginal English and the law: Communicating with Aboriginal English speaking clients: A handbook for legal practitioners*. Armidale, New South Wales: The Continuing Legal Education Department of the Queensland Law Soceity.

Eades, D. (1993). The case for Condren: Aboriginal English, pragmatics and the law. *Journal of Pragmatics, 20*, 141-162.

Eades, D. (1994a). A case of communicative clash: Aboriginal English and the legal system. In J. Gibbons (Ed.) *Language and the law*, (pp. 234-264). London: Longman Press.

Eades, D. (1994b). Forensic linguistics in Australia: An overview. *Forensic Linguistics, 1*(2), 113-132.

Eades, D. (1994c). They don't speak an Aboriginal language, or do they? In I. Keen (Ed.) *Being black: Aboriginal cultures in settled Australia*. Canberra: Aboriginal Studies Press.

Eades, D. (1995). *Language in evidence: Issues confronting Aboriginal and multicultural Australia*. Sydney, Australia: University of New South Wales Press.

Eades, D. (1996). Legal recognition of cultural differences in communication: The case of Robin Kina. *Language and Communication, 16*, 215-227.

Eades, D. (2000). *'I don't think it's an answer to the question'*: Silencing Aboriginal witnesses in court. *Language in Society, 29*, 161-195.

Eades, D. (2002). The politics of misunderstanding in the legal process: Aboriginal English in Queensland. In G. K. S. R. J. House

(Ed.) *Misunderstanding in spoken discourse*, (pp. 196-223). London: Longman.

Eades, D. (2003a). Participation of second language and second dialect speakers in the legal system. *Annual Review of Applied Linguistics, 23*, 113-133.

Eades, D. (2003b). "I don't think the lawyers were communicating with me": Misunderstanding cultural differences in communicative style. *Emory Law Journal, 52*, 1109-1134.

Eisenberg, L. (1977). Disease and illness: Distinctions between professional and popular ideas of sickness. *Culture, Medicine, and Psychiatry, 1*, 9-23.

Eisenberg, L., & Kleinman, A. (1981). *The relevance of social science for medicine*. Dordrecht, Holland: D. Reidel Publishing Co.

Emerson, R. M., Fretz, R. I., & Shaw, L. L. (1995). *Writing ethnographic field notes*. Chicago: The University of Chicago Press.

England, C. R. (n.d.). A look at the Indian Health Service policy of sterilization, 1972-1976. Retrieved June 31, 2004, from http://www.dickshovel.com/IHSSterPol.html

Erickson, F. (1979). Talking down: Some cultural sources of miscommunication in interracial interviews. In A. Wolfgang (Ed.) *Nonverbal behaviour*, (pp. 99-126). New York: Academic Press.

Ervin-Tripp, S. M. (1968). An analysis of the interaction of language, topic and listener. In J. Fishman (Ed.) *Readings in the Sociology of language*, (pp. 192-211). The Hague: Mouton & Co.

Fadiman, A. (1997). *The spirit catches you and you fall down: A Hmong child, her American doctors, and the collision of two cultures*. New York: Farrar, Straus and Giroux.

Farmer, P. (1982). Bad blood, spoiled milk—bodily fluids as moral barometers in rural Haiti. *American Ethnology, 15*(1), 62-83.

Farmer, P. (2003). *Pathologies of power: Health, human rights, and the new war on the poor*. Berkeley, CA: University of California Press.

Fiscella, K., Franks, P., Gold, M. R., & Clancy, C. M. (2000). Inequality in quality: Addressing the socioeconomic, racial, and ethnic disparities in health care. *Journal of the American Medical Association, 283*(19), 2579-2584.

Fishman, J. A. (1966). *Language loyalty in the United States*. The Hague: Mouton.

Fishman, J. A. (Ed.). (1968). *Readings in the Sociology of language*. The Hague: Mouton.

Fixico, D. L. (1998). *The invasion of Indian country in the twentieth century: American capitalism and tribal natural resources*. Niwot, CO: University Press of Colorado.

Fixico, D. L. (2003). *The American Indian mind in a linear world*. New York: Routledge.

Foucault, M. (1980). *Power/knowledge: Selected interviews & other writings, 1972-1977*. (trans. C. Gordon). New York: Pantheon Books.

Foucault, M. (1984). The order of discourse. In M. Shapiro (Ed.) *Critical language awareness*. New York: New York University Press.

Foucault, M. (1994 [1973]). *The birth of the clinic: An archaeology of medical perception*. (trans. A. M. S. Smith). New York: Vintage Books.

Foucault, M. (2004). "Je suis un artificier." In Roger-Pol Droit (Ed.) Odile Jacob, p. 95. (Interview conducted in 1975. (trans. Clare O'Farrell). Paris: Michel Foucault, entretiens.

Francis, V., & Korsch, M. (1969). Gaps in doctor-patient communication: Patient response to medical advice. *New England Journal of Medicine, 280*, 535-540.

Frankenberg, R. (1980). Medical anthropology and development: A theoretical perspective. *Social Science & Medicine, 14*(B), 197-207.

Frantz, K. (1999). *Indian reservations in the United States: Territory, sovereignty, and socioeconomic change*. Chicago: The University of Chicago Press.

Fuller, J. H. S., & Toon, P. D. T. (1988). *Medical practice in a multicultural society*. Oxford: Heinemann Medical Books.

Galfarsoro, I. (1998). Symbolic violence and linguistic habitus in Pierre Bourdieu: An instance of the 'language is power' view revisited.   Retrieved January 29, 2005, from http://ibs.lgu.ac.uk/forum/langx.htmhttp://ibs.lgu.ack.uk/forum/brindex.htm

Garrity, T. F. (1981). Medical compliance and the clinician-patient relationship: A review. *Social Science & Medicine, 15*(3), 215-222.

Geertz, C. (1973). *Interpretation of culture*. New York: Basic Books.

Giger, J. N., & Davidhizar, R. E. (1999). *Transcultural nursing: Assessment and intervention*. 3rd ed. St. Louis, MO: Mosby.

Giglioli, P. P. (1972). *Language and social context*. Baltimore, MD: Penguin Modern Sociology Readings.

Goffman, E. (1961). *Encounters: Two studies in the Sociology of interaction*. Indianapolis, IN: The Bobbs-Merrill Company.

Goffman, E. (1963). *Behavior in public places: Notes on the social organization of gatherings*. New York: The Free Press.

Goffman, E. (1964). The neglected situation. *The Ethnography of Communication, 66*(6, Part 2), 133-136.

Goffman, E. (1967). *Interaction ritual: Essays on face-to-face behavior*. Doubleday Anchor.

Goffman, E. (1969). *Strategic interaction*. Philadelphia: University of Pennsylvania Press.

Goffman, E. (1973). *The presentation of self in everyday life*. Woodstock, NY: The Overlook Press.

Goffman, E. (1981). *Forms of talk*. Philadelphia: University of Pennsylvania Press.

Goodyear-Smith, F., Buetow, F., & Buetow, S. (2001). Power issues in the doctor-patient relationship. *Health Care Analysis, 9,* 449-462.

Goulet, J.-G. (1998). *Ways of knowing: Experience, knowledge, and power among the Dene Tha*. Lincoln, NE: University of Nebraska Press.

Graham, A., & McDonald, J. (1997, November 28, 2004). Ethical principles for the conduct of research in the north. Retrieved July 29, 2004, from http://www.yukoncollege.yk.ca/~agraham/ethics.htm

Grande, S. (2004). *Red pedagogy: Native American social and political thought*. Lanham: Rowman & Littlefield Publishers.

Greco, M., Sweeney, K., Broomhall, J., & Beasley, P. (2001). Patient assessment of interpersonal skills: A clinical governance activity for hospital doctors and nurses. *Journal of Clinical Excellence, 3,* 117-124.

Gumperz, J. J. (1961). Speech variation and the study of Indian civilization. *American Anthropologist, 63*(5, Part 1), 976-988.

Gumperz, J. J. (1964). Linguistic and social interaction in two communities. *American Anthropologist, 66*(6, Part 2), 137-153.

Gumperz, J. J. (1968). Types of linguistic communities. In J. Fishman (Ed.) *Readings in the Sociology of language*, (pp. 460-472). The Hague: Mouton & Co.

Gumperz, J. J. (1972b). The speech community. In P. P. Giglioli (Ed.) *Language and social context*, (pp. 219-231). New York: Penguin.

Gumperz, J. J. (1978). The conversational analysis of interethnic communication. In E. L. Ross (Ed.) *Interethnic communication: Proceedings of the southern anthropological society*, (pp. 13-31). Georgia: University of Georgia Press.

Gumperz, J. J. (1979). Contextualization revisited. In *Contextualization of language*. Amsterdam: J. Benjamins.

Gumperz, J. J. (1982a). *Discourse strategies: Studies in interactional sociolinguistics 1*. Cambridge: Cambridge University Press.

Gumperz, J. J. (Ed.). (1982b). *Language and social identity: Studies in interactional sociolinguistics* (Vol. 2). Cambridge: Cambridge University Press.

Gumperz, J. J., & Hymes, D. (Eds.). (1972a). *Directions in sociolinguistics: The ethnography of communication*. Oxford: Basil Blackwell Ltd.

Gumperz, J. J., & Levinson, S. C. (1996). *Rethinking linguistic relativity*. Cambridge: Cambridge University Press.

Hahn, R. A. (1994). Rethinking 'illness' and 'disease'. *Contributions to Asian Studies*, *18*, 1-23.

Hahn, R. A. (1995). *Sickness and healing: An anthropological perspective*. New Haven, CT: Yale University Press.

Hall, E. T. (1966). Adumbration as a feature if intercultural communication. *The American Anthropologist*, *6*, 154-163.

Hall, E. T. (1969). *The hidden dimension: An anthropologist examines man's use of space in public and private*. Garden City, NY: Anchor Books.

Hall, E. T. (1976). *Beyond culture*. Garden City, NY: Anchor Books.

Hall, E. T. (1990). *The silent language*. New York: Anchor Books.

Hall, E. T., & Hall, M. (1990). *Understand cultural differences: German, French, Americans*. Yarmouth, ME: Intercultural Press.

Hall, E. T., & Whyte, W. F. (1960). Intercultural communication: A guide to men of action. *Human Organization, 19*(1), 5-12.

Hall, J. A., Roter, D. L., & Katz, N. R. (1988). Meta-analysis of correlates of provider behavior in medical encounters. *Medical Care, 28*(7), 657-675.

Hammersley, M., & Atkinson, P. (1995). *Ethnography: Principles in practice*. 2nd ed. London: Tavistock.

Hampton, J. R., Harrison, M. J. G., & Mitchell, J. R. H. (1975). Relative contributions of history taking, physical examination, and laboratory investigations to diagnosis and management of medical outpatients. *British Medical Journal, 2*, 486-489.

Hanks, W. F. (1993). Notes on semantics in linguistic practice. In C. Calhoun, E. LiPuma & M. Postone (Eds.), *Bourdieu: Critical perspectives*, (pp. 139-155). Chicago: University of Chicago Press.

Hanks, W. F. (2000). *Intertexts: Writings on language, utterance, and context*. Lanham, MD: Rowman & Littlefield.

Harrod, H. L. (2000). *The animals came dancing: Native American sacred ecology and animal kinship*. Tucson, AZ: The University of Arizona Press.

Haug, M. R., & Lavin, B. (1981). Practitioner or patient: Who's in charge. *Journal of Health and Social Behavior*, *22*(3), 212-229.

Helman, C. G. (1995). *Culture, health and illness*. 3rd ed. London: Butterworth-Heinemann.

Helman, C. G. (2000). *Culture, health and illness*. 4th ed. Cambridge: Oxford University Press.

Henderson, L. J. (1935). Physician and patient as a social system. *New England Journal of Medicine*, *212*, 819-823.

Hodes, R. (1997). Cross-cultural medicine and diverse health beliefs: Ethiopians abroad. *Western Journal of Medicine*, *166*, 29-36.

Hodgkinson, H. L. (1990). The demographics of American Indians: One percent of the people; fifty percent of the diversity. Washington, DC: Institute for Educational Leadership, Inc., Center for Demographic Policy.

Hulka, B. S., Cassel, J. C., Kupper, L. L., & Burdette, J. A. (1976). Communication compliance and concordance between physicians and patients with prescribed medications. *American Journal of Public Health*, *64*, 847-853.

Hymes, D. (1967). Models of the interaction of language and social setting. *Journal of Social Issues*, *23*(2).

Hymes, D. (1974a). *Foundations in sociolinguistics: An ethnographic approach*. Philadelphia: University of Pennsylvania Press.

Hymes, D. H. (1962). The ethnography of speaking. In J. Fishman (Ed.) *Readings in the Sociology of language*, (pp. 99-138). The Hague: Mouton & Co.

Hymes, D. H. (1972). Models of the interaction of language and social life. In J. J. Gumperz & D. H. Hymes (Eds.), *Directions in sociolinguistics: The ethnography of communication*, (pp. 35-71). New York: Hold, Rinehart, & Winston.

Hymes, D. H. (1974b). Ways of speaking. In R. Baumanm & J. Sherzer (Eds.), *Explorations in the ethnography of speaking*, (pp. 433-451). Cambridge: Cambridge University Press.

Hymes, D. H. (Ed.). (1964). *Language in culture and society: A reader in linguistics and anthropology*. New York: Harper & Rowe.

Jackson, J. L., Chamberlin, J., & Kroenke, K. (2001). Predictors of patient satisfaction. *Social Science & Medicine, 52*, 609-620.

Jain, N., & Kussmanin, E. D. (1997). Dominant cultural-patterns of Hindus in India. In L. A. Samovar & R. E. Portner (Eds.), *Intercultural communication: A reader*, (8th Ed.), (pp. 89-97). Belmont, CA: Wadsworth.

Kaplan, S. H., Breenfield, S., & Ware, J. E. (1989). Impact of the doctor-patient relationship on the outcomes of chronic diseases. In M. A. Stewart & D. L. Roter (Eds.), *Communicating with medical patients*. Newbury Park, CA: Sage.

Katz, J. (1984). *The silent world of doctor and patient*. Baltimore, MD: The Johns Hopkins University Press.

Kawagley, O. (1995). *A Yupiaq worldview: A pathway to ecology and spirit*. Prospects Heights, IL: Waveland Press.

Kenagy, J. W., Berwick, D. M., & Shore, M. F. (1999). Service quality in health care. *Journal of the American Medical Association, 281*(7), 661-665.

Kendon, A. (1967). Some functions of gaze-direction in social interaction. *Acta Psychologia, 26*, 22-63.

Kleinman, A. (1973a). Medicine's symbolic reality: On a central problem in the philosophy of medicine. *Inquiry: An Interdisciplinary Journal of Philosophy and the Social Sciences, 16*, 203-216.

Kleinman, A. (1973b). Toward a comparative study of medical systems: An integrated approach to the study of the relationship of medicine and culture. *Science, Medicine and Man, 1*, 55-65.

Kleinman, A. (1974). Cognitive structures of traditional medical systems: Ordering, explaining, and interpreting the human experience of illness. *Ethnomedism, III*(1/2), 27-49.

Kleinman, A. (1980). *Patients and healers in the context of culture: An exploration of the borderland between anthropology, medicine, and psychiatry.* Berkeley: University of California Press.

Kleinman, A. (1995). *Writing at the margin: Discourse between anthropology and medicine.* Berkeley, CA: University of California Press.

Kleinman, A. (1998). *The illness narratives: Suffering, healing and the human condition.* USA: Basic Books.

Kleinman, A., Das, V., & Lock, M. (1996). *Social suffering.* Berkeley, CA: University of California Press.

Kleinman, A., Eisenberg, L., & Good, B. (1978). Culture. Illness, and care: Clinical lessons from anthropologic and cross-cultural research. *Annals of Internal Medicine, 88*, 251-258.

Kleinman, A., & Sung, L. H. (1979). Why do indigenous practitioners successfully heal? *Social Science & Medicine, 13b*, 7-26.

Klopf, D. W. (1991). *Intercultural encounters: The fundamentals of intercultural communication.* 2nd ed. Englewood, CO: Morton Publishing Company.

Knapp, M. L. (1972). *Nonverbal communication in human interaction.* New York: Holt, Rinehart and Winston, Inc.

Korsch, B. M., Gozzi, E. K., & Francis, V. (1968). Gaps in doctor-patient communication: Doctor-patient interaction and patient satisfaction. *Pediatrics, 42*, 855-871.

Korsch, B. M., & Negrete, V. F. (1981). Doctor-patient communication. In G. Henderson (Ed.) *Physician-patient communication:
Readings and recommendations.* Springfield, IL: Thomas.

Kyasanur, N. M. (1987). Forest disease: An ethnography of a disease of development. *Medical Anthropology Quarterly, 1,* 406-
423.

Labov, W. (1964). The reflection of social processes in linguistic
structures. In J. Fishman (Ed.) *Readings in the Sociology of language,* (pp. 240-251). The Hague: Mouton & Co.

Labov, W. (1972). *Sociolinguistic patterns.* Philadelphia: University of Pennsylvania Press.

Laduke, W. (1999). *All our relations: Native struggles for land
and life.* Cambridge, MA: South End Press.

Lame Deer, J. F., & Erdoes, R. (1972). *Lame Deer: Seeker of visions.* New York: Washington Square Press.

Lane, S. D. (1983). Compliance, satisfaction, and physician-patient
communication. In R. Bostrom (Ed.) *Communication yearbook,*
Vol. 7, (pp. 772-799). Beverly Hills, CA: Sage.

Lang, F., & Huillen, J. H. (2000). The evolving roles of patient and
physician. *Archives of Family Medicine, 9,* 65-67.

Lantz, P. M., House, J. S., & Pepkowski, J. M. (1998). Socioeconomic factors, health behaviors, and mortality. *Journal of the
American Medical Association, 279,* 1703-1708.

Lawrence, J. (2002). The Indian health service and the sterilization
of Native American women. *American Indian Quarterly, 24*(3).

Leap, W. L. (1993). *American Indian English.* Salt Lake City, UT:
University of Utah Press.

Liberman, K. (1981). Understand Aboriginees in Australian courts
of law. *Human Organization, 40*(3), 247-255.

Lipkin, M., Jr. (1994). The medical interview and related skills. In W. T. Branch (Ed.) *Office practice of medicine*, (pp. 1287-1306). Philadelphia: WB Saunders Co.

Lipkin, M., Jr., Quill, T., & Napodano, R. J. (1984). The medical interview: A core curriculum for residencies in internal medicine. *Annals of Internal Medicine, 100*, 277-284.

Lobo, S., & Peters, K. (2001). *American Indians and the urban experience*. Walnut Creek, CA: Altamira Press.

Loustaunau, M. O., & Sobo, E. J. (1997). *The cultural context of health, illness, and medicine*. Westport, CT: Bergin & Garvey.

Luban-Plozza, B. (1995). Empowerment techniques: From doctor-centered (balint approach) to patient-centered discussion groups. *Patient Education and Counseling, 26*, 257-263.

Luckmann, J. (2000). *Transcultural communication in health care*. Africa: Delmar Thomson Learning.

Lustig, M. W., & Koester, J. (1999). *Intercultural competence: Interpersonal communication across cultures*. 3rd ed. New York: Longman.

Marvel, M. K., Epstein, R. M., Flowers, K. f., & Beckman, H. B. (1999). *Journal of the American Medical Association, 181*(3), 283-287.

Mathews, J. J. (1983). The communication process in clinical settings. *Social Science & Medicine, 17*(18), 1371-1378.

Matiella, A. C. (1994). *The multicultural challenge in health education*. Santa Cruz, CA: ETR Associates.

Mayberry, R. M., Mili, F., & Ofili, E. (2000). Racial and ethnic differences in access to medical care. *Medical Care Research and Review, 57*(1), 108-145.

McCleary, T. P. (1997). *The stars we know: Crow Indian astronomy and lifeways*. Prospect Heights, IL: Waveland Press.

Mead, N., & Bower, P. (2000). Patient-centeredness: A conceptual framework and review of the empirical literature. *Social Science & Medicine, 51*, 1087-1110.

Merkel, W. T. (1984). Physician perception of patient satisfaction: Do doctors know which patients are satisfied? *Medical Care, 22*(5), 453-459.

Mihesuah, D. A. (1996). *American Indians: Stereotypes and realities*. Clarity International. Atlanta, GA: Clarity Press.

Mihesuah, D. A. (1998). *Natives and academics: Researching and writing about Native Americans*. Lincoln, NE: University of Nebraska Press.

Mihesuah, D. A., & Wilson, A. C. (Eds.). (2004). *Indigenizing the academy: Transforming scholarship and empowering communities*. Lincoln: University of Nebraska Press.

Montoya, M. E. (2000). Silence and silencing: Their centripetal and centrifugal forces in legal communication, pedagogy and discourse. *Michigan Journal of Race & Law, 5*(Summer), 847-941.

Moore, M. (2003). *Genocide of the mind*. New York: Thunder's Mouth Press.

Murira, N., Lützen, K., Lindmark, G., & Christensson, K. (2003). Communication patterns between health care providers and their clients at an antenatal clinic in Zimbabwe. *Health Care for Women International, 24*, 83-92.

Murray, D. (2000). *Indian Giving: Economics of Power in Indian-White Exchanges*. Amherst: University of Massachusetts Press.

Nadar, L. (1996). *Naked science: An introduction for health professionals*. New York: Routledge Press.

Nason, J. D. (1996). Tribal models for controlling research. *Tribal College Journal, 8*, 17-20.

Navarro, V. (1985). U.S. Marxists' scholarship in the analysis of health and medicine. *International Journal of Health Services, 15*, 95-98.

O'Brien, S. (1989). *American Indian tribal governments*. Norman, OK: The University of Oklahoma Press.

Ong, A. (1995). Making the biopolitical subject: Cambodian immigrants, refugee medicine and cultural citizenship in California. *Social Science & Medicine, 40*(9), 1245-1257.

Osiatynski, W. (Ed.), *Contrasts: Soviet and American Thinkers Discuss the Future.* Noam Chomsky interviewed by Wiktor Osiatynski (pp. 95-101). MacMillan.

Paper, J. (1988). *Offering Smoke: The Sacred Pipe and Native American Religion.* Moscow, ID: University of Idaho Press.

Parsons, T. (1951). *The social system.* Glencoe, IL: Free Press.

Parsons, T. (1975). The sick role and the role of the physician reconsidered. *Milbank Memorial Fund Quarterly/Health and Society, 53*, 257-278.

Peabody, F. (1988 [1976]). The care of the patient. *Connecticut Medicine, 40*, 545.

Peacock, T. D. (1996). Issues in American Indian research: The perspective of a reservation Indian, American Indian Research Symposium. Orcas Island, WA: University of Minnesota, Deluth.

Peat, D. F. (1994). *Blackfoot physics: A journey into the Native American universe.* Grand Rapids, MI: Phanes Press.

Pennycock, A. (2001). *Critical applied linguistics: A critical introduction.* Mahwah, N.J., London: Lawrence Erlbaum.

Philips, S. U. (1974). Warm Springs 'Indian time': How the regulation of participation affects the progression of events. In R. Bauman & J. Sherzer (Eds.), *Explorations in the exploration of ethnography of speaking*, (pp. 92-109). Cambridge: Cambridge University Press.

Philips, S. U. (1983). *The invisible culture: Communication in classroom and community on the Warm Springs Indian reservation*. New York: Longman.

Pratt, L., Seligmann, A., & Reader, C. (1957). Physicians' views on the level of medical information among patients. *American Journal of Public Health*, 47(10), 1277-1283.

Red Horse, J., Shattuck, A., & Hoffman, F. (1980). The American Indian family: Strengths and stresses. Paper presented at the Conference on Research Issues, Phoenix, AZ.

Rehbein, J. (2001). Intercultural negotiation. In A. Di Luzio, S. Günthner & F. Orletti (Eds.), *Culture in communication: Analyses of intercultural situations*, (pp. 173-183). Amsterdam: John Benjamins.

Rich, A. (1974). *Interracial communication*. New York: Harper & Row.

Romney, K. A., & D'Andrade, R. (1966). Transcultural studies in cognition. *American Anthropologist*, 3(special issue).

Roter, D. L. (1989). Which facts of communication have strong effect on outcome: A meta-analysis. In M. Steward & D. L. Roter (Eds.), *Communicating with medical patients*. Newbury Park: Sage.

Roter, D. L., Hall, E. T., & Katz, J. A. (1987). Relations between physicians' behaviors and analogue patients' satisfaction, recall, and impressions. *Medical Care*, 25, 437-451.

Ryan, M.-L. (n.d.). Entry for the forthcoming *Routledge Encyclopedia of Narrative*. Retrieved November 7, 2004, from http://lamar.colostate.edu/~pwryan/narrentry.htm

Sandler, G. (1980). The importance of the history in the medical clinic and the cost of unnecessary tests. *American Heart Journal, 100*, 938-931.

Sanson-Fisher, R., & Maguire, P. (1980). Should skills in communicating with patients be taught in medical schools? *The Lancet*, September, 523-526.

Sarangi, S. (1994). Intercultural or not? Beyond celebration of cultural differences in miscommunication analysis. *International Pragmatics Association, 4*(3), 409-427.

Saville-Troike, M. (1985). The place of silence in an integrated theory of communication. In D. Tannen & M. Saville-Troike (Eds.), *Perspectives on silence*, (pp. 3-18). Westport, CN: Greenwood.

Scheper-Hughes, N. (1988). The madness of hunger: Sickness, delirium and human needs. *Culture, Medicine, and Psychiatry, 12*, 429-458.

Scheper-Hughes, N., & Lock, M. (1987). The mindful body: A prolegomenon to future work in medical anthropology. *Medical Anthropology Quarterly, 18*, 6-41.

Schmitz, U. (1994). Eloquent silence. Retrieved July 14, 2004, from http://www.linse.uni-essen.de/linse/publikationen/silence.html

Schwab, J. (1988). Ambiguity, style, and kinship in Adelaide Aboriginal identity. In I. Keen (Ed.) *Being black: Aboriginal cultures in 'settled' Australia*, (pp. 77-95). Canberra: Aboriginal Studies Press.

Scollon, R. (1985). The machine stops: Silence in the metaphor of malfunction. In D. Tannen & M. Saville-Troike (Eds.), *Perspectives on silence*, (pp. 21-30). Westport, CT: Greenwood.

Segall, A. (1976). Sociocultural variations in sick role behavioral expectations. *Social Science & Medicine, 10*, 47-51.

Sharf, B. F. (1988). Teaching patients to speak up: Past and future trends. *Patient Education and Counseling, 11*, 95-108.

Sherzer, J. (1987). A discourse-centered approach to language and culture. *American Anthropologist, 89*, 295-309.

Shoemaker, N. (2002). *Clearing a path: Theorizing the past in Native American studies.* New York: Routledge.

Shorter, E. (1985). *Bedside manners.* New York: Simon and Schuster.

Simons-Morton, D. G., Mullen, P. D., Mains, D. A., Tabak, E. R., & Green, I. (1992). Characteristics of controlled studies of patient educations and counseling for preventive health behaviors. *Patient Education and Counseling, 19*, 175-204.

Simpson, M., Buckman, R., M., S., Maguire, P., Lipkin, M., Jr., & Novak, D. (1991). Doctor-patient communication: The Toronto consensus statement. *British Medical Journal, 303*, 1385-1387.

Singer, M. (1986). Developing a critical perspective in medical anthropology. *Medical Anthropology Quarterly, 17*, 128-129.

Singer, M. (1989). Keep the label and the perspective: A response to 'emic' critiques of medical anthropology. *Anthropology Newsletter, 1989*(March), 15-19.

Slobin, D. I. (Ed.). (1967). *A field manual for cross-cultural study of the acquisition of communicative competence.* Berkeley, CA: University of California Press.

Slobin, K. (1998). Healing through the use of symbolic technologies among the Dogon of Mali. *High Plains Applied Anthropologist*, *17*(2), 136-143.

Smith, A. L. (1973). *Transracial communication*. Englewood Cliffs: Prentice Hall.

Smith, L. T. (1999). *Decolonizing methodologies: Research and indigenous people*. London: Zed Books, Ltd.

Smyth, J., Gould, O., & Solobin, K. (2000). The role of narrative medicine: A multi-theoretical perspective. *Advances in Mind and Body Medicine*, *16*(3), 199-207.

Snow, L. F. (1993). *Walkin' over medicine*. Boulder, CO: Westview Press.

Sorlie, P. D., Backlund, E., & Keller, J. B. (1995). US mortality by economic, demographic, and social characteristics. *American Journal of Public Health*, *85: 949-956.*

Spacks, P. M. (1985). *Gossip*. New York: Alfred A. Knoff.

Speedling, E. J. a. D. N. R. (1985). Building an effective doctor-patient relationship: From patient satisfaction to patient participation. *Social Science & Medicine*, *21*(2), 115-120.

Spiro, D., & Heidrich, F. (1983). Lay understanding of medical terminology. *The Journal of Family Practice*, *17*, 277-279.

Stewart, M. (1991). Effective patient-physician communication and health outcomes: A review. *Canadian Medical Association Journal*, *303*, 423-433.

Stewart, M., Brown, J., J., L., McCracken, E., & McWhinney, I. R. (1986). The patient-centered clinical method: Changes in residents' performance over two months of training. *Family Practice*, *3*, 164-167.

Stewart, M. A. (1984). What is a successful doctor-patient interview? A study of interactions and outcomes. *Social Science & Medicine, 19*(2), 167-175.

Street, R. L. (1991). Information-giving in medical consultations: The influence of patients' communicative styles and personal characteristics. *Social Science & Medicine, 32*(5), 541-548.

Stubbs, P. (1993). *'Ethnically sensitive' or 'anti-racist'? Models for health research and service delivery*. Buckingham: Open Universe.

Suchman, A. L., & Matthews, D. A. (1988). What makes the patient-doctor relationship therapeutic? Exploring the connexional dimension of medical care. *Annals of Internal Medicine, 108*, 125-130.

Suchman, E. A. (1965). Social patterns of illness and medical care. *Journal of Health and Human Behavior, 6*, 114-128.

Svarstad, B. (1999). Physician-patient communication and patient conformity with medical advice. *New England Journal of Medicine, 37*(11), 1169-1173.

Swartz, D. (1997). *Culture and power: The Sociology of Pierre Bourdieu*. Chicago: University of Chicago Press.

Szasz, T., & Hollender, M. H. (1956). A contribution of the philosophy of medicine: The basic models of the doctor-patient relationship. *Archives of Internal Medicine, 97*, 585-592.

Tafoya, T. (1989). Circles and cedar: Native Americans and family therapy. *Journal of Psychotherapy and the Family, 61*, 71-98.

Tannen, D., & Saville-Troike, M. (1985a). Silence: Anything but. In D. Tannen & M. Saville-Troike (Eds.), *Perspectives on silence*, (pp. 93-109). Westport, CT: Greenwood Publishing Group, Incorporated.

Tannen, D., & Saville-Troike, M. (Eds.). (1985b). *Perspectives on silence*. Westport, CN: Greenwood.

Thompson, D., & Ciecbanowski, P. S. (2003). Attaching a new understanding to the patient-physician relationship in family practice. *Journal of the American Board of Family Practice, 16*, 219-226.

Thornton, R. (1998). *Studying Native America: Problems and prospects*. Madison, Wisconsin: The University of Wisconsin Press.

Toffler, A. (1990). *Powershift: Knowledge, wealth and violence at the edge of the 21st century*. New York: Bantam Books.

Trafzer, C. E., & Weiner, D. (2001). *Medicine ways: Disease, health, and survival among Native Americans*. Walnut Creek, CA: AltaMira Press.

Trimble, J. E., & Medicine, B. (1993). Diversification of American Indians: Forming an indigenous perspective. In U. Kim & J. W. Berry (Eds.), *Indigenous psychologies: Research and experience in cultural context*, (pp. 133-151). Newbury Park, CA: Sage.

University of Manitoba. (n. d.). Culture. Retrieved February 17, 2005, from http://www.tamu.edu/classes/cosc/choudhurry/culture.html

Ventres, W., & Gordon, P. (1990). Communication strategies in caring for the underserved. *Journal of Health Care for the Poor and Underserved, 1*, 305-314.

Waitzkin, H. (1985). Information giving in medical care. *Journal of Health and Social Behavior, 26*(2), 81-101.

Waitzkin, H. (1986). Micropolitics of medicine: Theoretical issues. *Medical Anthropology Quarterly, 17*, 134-135.

Waitzkin, H. (1989). A critical theory of medical discourse: Ideology, social control, and the processing of social context in medical encounters. *Journal Of Health and Social Behavior, 30*(3), 220-239.

Waters, A. (Ed.). (2004). *American Indian thought: Philosophical essays*. Malden, MA: Blackwell.

Weatherford, J. (1988), Indian Givers: How the Indians of the Americas Transformed the World. New York, Fawcett Books.

Weaver, H. (1997). The challenges of research in Native American communities: Incorporating principles of cultural competence. *Journal of Social Service Research, 23*(2), 1-15.

Webber, G. C. (1990). Patient education: A review of the issues. *Medical Care, 28*, 1089-1103.

Wilkens, D. E., & Lomawaima, K. T. (2001). *Uneven ground: American Indian sovereignty and federal law*. Norman, OK: University of Oklahoma Press.

Williams, R. A. (1997). *Linking arms together: American Indian treaty visions of law and peace, 1600-1800*. New York: Routledge Press.

Woloshin, S., Bickwell, N., & Schwartz, L. (1995). Language barriers in medicine in the United States. *Journal of the American Medical Association, 273*(9), 724-728.

Woolley, F. R., Kane, R. L., Hughes, C. C., & Wright, D. D. (1978). The effects of the doctor-patient communication of satisfaction and outcome of care. *Social Science & Medicine, 12*, 123-128.

Zeuschner, R. (1997). *Communicating today*. 2nd ed. Boston: Allyn & B

Made in the USA
Monee, IL
16 October 2024

68086016R00125